A CLOSER WALK

DEVOTIONS BY
STEVE TROXEL

VOLUME 1

A CLOSER WALK
Volume I

Published by

God's Daily Word Ministries
http://www.gdwm.org

ISBN 0-9708531-4-9
Copyright © 2004
by
God's Daily Word Ministries.
First Printing October 2003
Second Printing October 2004

Written by Steve Troxel

Cover Design by Al Mendenhall
Creative Vision Studio, San Antonio, Texas

Printed in Canada

CONTENTS

CONTENTS

PREFACE

In August of 1996, as my wife and I were on the way to the hospital for the birth of our daughter, I sent a short email to a few friends and family. Unaware at the time, this was the beginning of God's Daily Word Ministries. The updates on my daughter's birth changed to short words of encouragement and scripture verses, and later grew to full devotionals.

Over the last several years, God has led thousands of people from all over the world to be a part of this growing ministry. This has been a wonderful journey of ever increasing faith and trust.

God has taught me that His main message is a continuous call to draw nearer and to love and trust Him more. This is His message when He first calls us to believe in Jesus for the forgiveness of sin and be restored to a relationship which has been broken for so long. It's also His message when we have journeyed with Him for a long while but are continuously subject to the pulls of the world.

This book is intended to be the first volume of a six volume set. The devotional messages in each of these books are written to give some instruction from God's Word as well as application and encouragement to draw nearer to God through trust, love and worship. These messages are for those who are seeking as well as those who have trusted Jesus for many years. I firmly believe that, no matter where we are in our relationship with God, we ALL are being called to A Closer Walk!

Steve Troxel

RESOLVE TO BE TRANSFORMED

What will we do different this year? There are more resolutions made during the first week of January than at any other time of the year - more diets are begun and more attempts at various forms of self-improvement. I confess I made a resolution to run one thousand miles this year. I'll also confess I'm not off to a great start - I've only run two miles in the first five days. [Note: This message was written on January 6th, 2003. I ran my 1000th mile on September 15th and ended the year with 1508 miles. Praise God!!]

No matter when this message is actually being read, today is the beginning of a new year. Most good-intended resolutions will soon be forgotten, but some will make lasting changes for the better. If it takes the commitment of a "New Year" resolution to break free of a bad habit, restore a broken relationship or improve your health, then by all means resolve!

But as we reflect on the past and excitedly plan for the future, let's focus our effort on changes which have eternal significance. Jesus said it well as He admonished the Pharisees: "You clean the outside of the cup and dish, but inside they are full of greed and self-indulgence. First clean the inside...and then the outside also will be clean" (Matthew 23:25-26).

1

The Bible speaks about the initial transformation which occurs when we become a "new creation" in Christ. But it also speaks about the on-going transformation as we draw closer to God and achieve the peace and contentment found only in His presence.

Romans 12:2

"Do not conform any longer to the pattern of this world, but be transformed by the renewing of your mind. Then you will be able to test and approve what God's will is - His good, pleasing and perfect will."

The renewing of our mind is an inward change where we are "conformed to the likeness of His Son" (Romans 8:29). It's a process of changing our thoughts, priorities, and goals to be aligned with those of Christ; "Let this mind be in you, which was also in Christ Jesus" (Philippians 2:5 KJV). The mind of Christ was pure, focused on the Father, and determined to do His will; "My food is to do the will of Him who sent Me and to finish His work" (John 4:34).

On our list of things to do different this next year, I pray we include more time with God in prayer, more time in His Word, more time loving Him with ALL our heart, seeking His presence, and earnestly desiring to know, and do, His will. Let our prayer for one another be that we draw ever closer to our Heavenly Father and experience His love new and fresh every day. In this new year, let's make eternal resolutions as we resolve to be transformed!

ONLY ONE IS NEEDED

The news is filled with stories of pain and heartache, of frustration and confusion. It seems everywhere we turn, people are crying out for help and simply existing from day to day. This is NOT the life God intended! The abundance of trials we see today is not necessarily a reflection of a drastic change in the world; rather, it's likely the result of our eyes being opened and our heart becoming more sensitive to His Spirit. This is a call which requires a bold response.

Over the last several years, God has performed a radical change in my life. I no longer see with the same eyes and my definition of "important" has been completely transformed. I try to live each day in submission to the Spirit of Christ and seek to glorify Him in all I do. The result has been a wonderful peace and contentment. I'm often overwhelmed with the blessings of God and can't help but praise Him for being set free.

But there are times I begin to doubt and become tentative with my message. I question whether the peace I've received is truly available to those who are in such pain. Can the miracle which occurred in my life really happen in the life of others? I now confess this doubt to you as sin! God has transformed my life and led me to this ministry for the purpose of proclaiming His truth: He came to set us free, but freedom is only found through submission and devotion.

Martha had become irritated that her sister Mary was sitting at the feet of Jesus rather than helping her prepare the meal. In fact, she was so bothered she approached Jesus and said: "Lord, don't You care that my sister has left me to do the work by myself? Tell her to help me!" (Luke 10:40). But Jesus very patiently replied:

Luke 10:41-42

"Martha, Martha, you are worried and upset about many things, but only one thing is needed. Mary has chosen what is better, and it will not be taken away from her."

The world continually tries to tell us what's necessary and important - but it's a lie! And we never really understand nor see the deception until we consistently make the time to worship at the feet of Jesus and hear Him say; "You have now chosen what is better."

No matter what this day may bring, we must live each and every moment in devotion to our Lord. No matter what our circumstances, we CAN be set free! We may need to adjust our priorities and eliminate some things which consume our time and clutter our thoughts; but true worship at His feet is worth it ALL. Let's take a stand for Christ, faithfully proclaim His truth to the world, and build our life on His solid foundation. Many things may seem important, but only one is needed!

NEW EVERY MORNING

God loved us so much that He gave His Son as a sacrifice for our sins, that through faith we might be brought back into a full and intimate relationship with our Heavenly Father for all eternity. I think we often forget the magnitude of this love: we were dead and He provided us a way to live!

Lamentations 3:22-23

> *"Because of the Lord's great love we are not consumed, for His compassions never fail. They are new every morning; great is Your faithfulness."*

God has expressed His absolute love and compassion through the forgiveness found in Jesus Christ. This forgiveness is total and complete for those who believe. When we place our trust in Jesus, we are washed clean - we become "a new creation; the old has gone, the new has come" (2 Corinthians 5:17). And we continue to be washed clean "every morning."

We all have days when our sinful nature wins a battle and we stumble. We have a day when our anger, pride, fear, or lust is brought to the surface and we "do what we do not want to do" (Romans 7:16). We may need to seek forgiveness and earn back trust from those we've hurt, but God's forgiveness and love is free for the asking; "If we confess our sins, He is faithful and just and will forgive us our sins" (1 John 1:9). We may lose some of the battles, but through Jesus, the war has been won.

Since we have been washed clean - and continue to be washed clean - we must stop walking as though we are still soiled. We are children of God and in the process of being conformed to the likeness of His Son. This process of growth and maturity - of victorious transformation - must continue each and every morning. We must shed the heavy burdens of past failures (and the fear of future disappointments) and walk in the freshness of His forgiveness.

Is our relationship with God fresh and new? Do we still comprehend the magnitude of love encompassed in the gift of forgiveness? Or have we grown complacent and cold? When was the last time our love for God was so fresh on our heart that we couldn't help but say THANK YOU!?

We are invited to a relationship with our Heavenly Father - an intimate relationship which involves loving and being loved; a relationship which allows us to walk in victory for His glory and to be guided by the power of His Spirit. Let's give Him our all and receive His all in return. Let's rise up in His strength and determine to make our relationship of love new every morning.

FOUNDATION OF TRUTH

Six hundred years ago, there were groups of people who believed the earth was flat. In fact they didn't just believe the earth was flat, they "knew" the earth was flat. Because of this belief, they also believed it was impossible to sail round the world. Of course, their view was warped and limited since it was built upon knowledge which was not based in truth.

What knowledge and "facts" form our view of the world today? We probably have a better understanding of the physical workings of our world, but what knowledge determines how we view our life? Do we begin with the unlimited power and sovereignty of God, an understanding of eternity, the consequences of sin, and the saving grace of Jesus Christ?

If we allow our beliefs to be formed by the world system, our view of life will always remain limited. Rather than seeing God's loving hand at work in our life and clearly recognizing His tools of transformation, we will see only unnecessary suffering and the apparent absence of God; "The fear {or holy reverence} of the Lord is the beginning of knowledge" (Proverbs 1:7).

Clearly, God is calling us to a closer and more meaningful relationship: calling us to love Him and trust Him more. But we will never

7

truly grow closer until we examine the foundation of our beliefs; "In the beginning, God created the heavens and the earth" (Genesis 1:1). The entire Universe, and certainly our life, was formed by God and continues to exist because of His grace. To believe anything less is to fail to understand God and fail to believe His Word.

Spiritual understanding is gained through the guidance and power of the Holy Spirit as we diligently pray and study God's Word. Initially, our prayers may seem empty and His Word full of disjoint stories which don't seem to apply; but if we continue to seek with all our heart, He will reveal His truth and we will soon begin to understand.

Proverbs 2:3-5

"If you call out for insight and cry aloud for understanding, and if you look for it as for silver and search for it as for hidden treasure, then you will understand the fear of the Lord and find the knowledge of God."

God has gifted us with the ability to learn, the power to seek, and the freedom to choose how we use our time. Let's use His gift to find the knowledge of God based on the reverence of His name. Let's build a world view which is consistent with God's Word and will stand the test of eternity. Let's refuse to limit God, and forevermore base our lives on the foundation of truth.

CLEAR LINE OF COMMUNICATION

Communication is a key part of any relationship. Without proper communication, a relationship will slowly drift apart and feel isolated. This is true of friends and married couples, and certainly true in our relationship with God.

Without communication, we begin to drift and will soon be unable to even recognize His voice. When faced with sudden burdens we will feel alone. We may awkwardly call out to God but find our communication line has become noisy, filled with distractions. It's difficult to receive direction or comfort when we can't even hear or understand what God is saying.

To keep the communication lines clear, we must develop the habit of continually talking with God; "Pray continually" (1 Thessalonians 5:17). We cannot limit prayer to those times of great need. David was in the habit of morning prayer; "In the morning, O Lord, You hear my voice; in the morning I lay my request before You and wait in expectation" (Psalm 5:3). But we must also learn to talk with God throughout our day so we are prepared for those times of extra need.

Jesus never suffered from a breakdown in communication with His Father; "I and the

Father are one" (John 10:30). And yet, when faced with major decisions or burdens, Jesus still set aside special time to talk with God.

Luke 6:12-13

> *"One of those days Jesus went out to a mountainside to pray, and spent the night praying to God. When morning came, He called His disciples to Him and chose twelve of them, whom He also designated apostles."*

There are always going to be times in our Christian walk where we need dedicated time with God - times which involve "critical" or "crisis" situations. This time is greatly enhanced if we have already been walking in daily communion with the Father. Our "crisis" prayers may be more intense and contain a heightened sense of urgency, but at least we will know the One to whom we pray - we will know His voice and understand His ultimate plan for our life.

Our Heavenly Father desires to light our path by giving daily guidance. Let's develop the habit of continual prayer so we will follow His leading and walk each step in praise. Let's KNOW Him during the trivial and mundane portion of our day so we will be prepared to know Him during the urgent. Let's prioritize our life to ensure we have a free and clear line of communication.

A LIVING SANCTUARY

Our Heavenly Father desires our life to be FILLED with praise and worship. When we gather together with other believers for church services, we generally begin with songs of praise. We praise God for His love and faithfulness, and for the gift of His Son. We worship Him for His awesome majesty as we prepare our hearts to receive His Word. These are wonderful times, but they are only a small part of God's true desire for our life.

Ephesians 5:19-20

"Speak to one another with psalms, hymns and spiritual songs. Sing and make music in your heart to the Lord, always giving thanks to God the Father for everything, in the name of our Lord Jesus Christ."

As Paul wrote these instructions to the Ephesians he never said, "give thanks only during your worship service," or, "make music in your heart only when you gather together with other believers." He clearly instructed "always" and "for everything." The "music" of praise and worship to God should always reside in our heart.

This can be a real challenge without a shift in the way we view our life - a shift from the way we've been "trained" by the world. We absolutely must learn to "trust in the Lord with all your heart and lean not on your own understanding" (Proverbs 3:5). Though the world teaches us to "take charge of your own destiny," we are called to release control to our Lord and patiently trust. For it's only through faith and trust that we can praise in ALL situations, even through our confusion and pain.

One of my favorite praise songs contains the words: "Lord prepare me to be a sanctuary; pure and holy, tried and true. With thanksgiving, I'll be a living sanctuary for You." The word sanctuary means: "A place set aside as sacred and holy, especially a place of worship." The meaning of this song then becomes: Lord prepare my life to be a sacred and holy place of worship!

There can be no greater ambition for the Child of God. With a proper understanding of eternity and the saving grace of Jesus, our life only has real purpose as we live each day to bring Him glory and honor - as we live each moment in praise and worship, no matter what circumstances our day may bring. The way we walk through our trials as well as how we accomplish our daily tasks, ministry activities, or times of prayer and study should all be done through a heart devoted to worship.

Let's allow the "music" of our heart to sing out with praise and worship - not just for a few set hours each week, but every day with every word, thought and deed. Let's patiently trust in all areas of our life and ask our Father to teach us to live as a living sanctuary.

HIS PERFECT WAY

In the message "A Living Sanctuary" we considered our call to praise and worship ALWAYS; and that this can only occur as we trust God with all our heart and release control into His hands. We seem to often come back to this theme - maybe it's because this is one of our major struggles.

The world definitely trains us to take control. There even seems to be special rewards for those who can say, "I did it my way!" But the truth is, "my" way will always fall short of God's desire. Our biggest struggle is often finding the balance which keeps us on His path and traveling at His pace. Lack of faith causes us to lag behind, and our pride and desire to control causes us to try and push ahead.

2 Samuel 22:31

"As for God, His way is perfect; the word of the Lord is flawless. He is a shield for all who take refuge in Him."

These words are part of a song of praise King David sang to God. Several times in his life David ventured out to do things his own way. Yet time after time he found that walking down God's path was not only the best way, it was the perfect way. We must obviously learn this same lesson. We are given many options -

many roads to travel as we seek a better way - but His narrow road is the only way to true life...the only road to peace and true contentment.

Living by God's way requires constant renewal of faith and trust. It first requires faith in Jesus for the forgiveness of sin, and then complete trust as we continue down His path. While God's way is definitely perfect, it's not always easy to understand. His way will often conflict with what we just "know" is best; "The man who thinks he knows something does not yet know as he ought to know" (1 Corinthians 8:2). These times of apparent conflict are times to humbly increase our faith and better learn how to trust.

But the "wisdom" of the world will continually battle against this trust. Jesus said, "do not worry about your life, what you will eat or drink; or about your body, what you will wear" (Matthew 6:25). The world's wisdom says we will soon be hungry and naked; but God's wisdom says that as we trust Him with all our heart, we will soon find rest and peace; "But seek first His kingdom and His righteousness, and all these things will be given to you as well" (Matthew 6:33).

God has gifted each of us in unique and wonderful ways. But our gifts must be used along His path, for His glory, or they become nothing but "filthy rags" (Isaiah 64:6). Let's stop seeking our way, with our goals and our desires. Instead, let's daily release to the guidance of the Holy Spirit and boldly follow where He leads. Let's trust and walk each and every step according to His perfect way.

THE EXAMINED LIFE

We've heard it said and it proves to be true: the unexamined life is not worth living. If we flow through life without evaluating who we are and what we believe, we have not really lived. Deep down, we all desire to take a stand and live according to a consistent set of beliefs. This requires a boldness to go beyond the surface and into our very soul! Without this boldness we may give the appearance of living, and may even fool ourselves for a number of years, but there will always be an emptiness until we look deep within and deal with what we find.

God knows every detail of our heart; "Everything is uncovered and laid bare before the eyes of Him to whom we must give account" (Hebrews 4:13). But our Heavenly Father desires for us to know what we believe as we are being transformed; "Examine yourselves to see whether you are in the faith; test yourselves" (2 Corinthians 13:5).

As we seek to understand our heart - with all our hidden motives, pride, and selfishness - we find we're somewhat difficult to understand. Without the Spiritual help which God freely gives, there will be parts of our life which remain covered and dark. There may also be portions of our heart we would rather not face.

15

Psalm 139:23-24

*"Search me, O God, and know my heart;
test me and know my anxious thoughts.
See if there is any offensive way in me,
and lead me in the way everlasting."*

It's foolishness to think we can hide anything from God! It's equally foolish to intentionally close areas of our heart from examination when we know what's inside is keeping us separated from God. What do we really believe? And are we living consistent with that belief?

We have been given God's Word as a guide; "a lamp to my feet" (Psalm 119:105). And as we dig deeper into His Word, we find the same lamp which guides our steps also reveals our heart: "The lamp of the Lord searches the spirit of a man; it searches out his inmost being" (Proverbs 20:27). Using God's Word to truly examine our heart can be painful. It seems we strip back one layer only to expose additional layers of sin we didn't even know we had; but this process must continue without fear!

If we desire to live in His presence and bring Him glory and honor in all we do, we must determine today to know ourselves. We must know what we believe, with all our strengths and weaknesses, and know our level of resolve to follow where He leads. Let's open our heart and allow His Spirit to search and wash us with His Word. Let's follow according to a consistent belief and commit to living the examined life.

WE WILL OVERCOME

God's Word contains many passages which encourage us in our struggles. Paul tells us to "press on toward the goal" (Philippians 3:14), "run a good race" (Galatians 5:7), and "fight the good fight" (2 Timothy 4:7). Each of these acknowledge the struggle and exhort us to keep moving forward. But there are times we become weary and even the thought of pressing, running, or fighting becomes difficult. Yet, we know we must endure - we must overcome!

Revelation 2:7

> *"He who has an ear, let him hear what the Spirit says to the churches. To him who overcomes, I will give the right to eat from the tree of life, which is in the paradise of God."*

In the second and third chapters of Revelation, the Apostle John is simply dictating the words spoken by Jesus. In these two chapters, Jesus speaks seven times about "him who overcomes." Each time there is a gift or reward for the one who is "successful" and overcomes. This is certainly good motivation for us to endure, but the question still remains: How can we overcome as our strength begins to fade?

John knew what it took to overcome. Several years earlier, he had written a letter to encourage believers to stay committed and to give the assurance of eternal life. He also specified exactly who would overcome: "Everyone born of God overcomes the world... Who is it that overcomes the world? Only he who believes that Jesus is the Son of God" (1 John 5:4-5). Read this carefully and rejoice! Those who believe are those who will overcome!!

We must endure and overcome the world; but our faith in Jesus and NOT our strength is was causes us to endure. There are times we must run and times we must fight - times we will be called to be a mighty warrior for the Lord. But there are also times when we are terribly weak - times we must grab on to Jesus and allow HIS strength to carry us through the storm. These are times we will need to simply hold on!

When the battle seems unbearable, "Hold on to what you have - I {Jesus} am coming soon" (Revelation 3:11). When we feel surrounded by evil and the darkness is closing in, "Hold on to the good" (1 Thessalonians 5:21). And when we become overwhelmed with doubt and fear, "Hold on to our courage and the hope of which we boast" (Hebrews 3:6).

When we are weary in the storm, let's take comfort in the peaceful waters ahead. Let's fix our eyes on Jesus and hold on...He will never let us go. He has given His Children a wonderful promise: as we continue to believe and trust Him with all our heart, we WILL overcome!

JOIN THE BATTLE

In the message "We Will Overcome" we were encouraged to hold on to Jesus when our strength fades and we become weary. We saw that our continued faith (not our strength) ensures we will overcome and receive the gift of eternal life. We can take great comfort in knowing Jesus will carry us and not let us fall; but we must also remember we were not born into His family to be permanently carried: "Those who hope in the Lord will renew their strength. They will soar on wings like eagles" (Isaiah 40:31). As we draw near to God through dedicated quiet times of prayer, He WILL renew our strength; and when He does, we must once again march into battle.

We often forget there's a war being fought all around us. We tend to become passive because we don't actually see the fighting. There are no official announcements of enemy strength and no news flashes of casualties. But make no mistake...it's a war!

Ephesians 6:12

"For our struggle is not against flesh and blood, but against the rulers, against the authorities, against the powers of this dark world and against the spiritual forces of evil in the heavenly realms."

Just as surely as there is a God who gave His Son to die for our sins, there is also a devil and spiritual forces doing battle. The good news is that we know the final outcome of this war; "And the devil, who deceived them, was thrown into the lake of burning sulfur" (Revelation 20:10).

The devil's end is certain; but in the meantime, he's on a mission to take as many with him as possible; "If anyone's name was not found written in the book of life, he was {also} thrown into the lake of fire" (Revelation 20:15). The stakes of this war are high. The enemy continues to attack and rejoices when we think we're defeated.

But we are NOT defeated! We may lose our focus; we may stray from what's really important and trust in things which are fading; we may even experience times of fear and doubt; but we are definitely not defeated! The road to victory has been placed at our feet. It begins with our next determined step of drawing closer to God and loving Him with all our heart.

As our strength returns (and it will!) we must pick up the Word of God and become a soldier! There are many all around us with deep wounds who are literally dying for help. Let's not be content to sit on the sidelines or be forever carried. Let's present our lives to God and allow Him to work through us to encourage others in their walk and share the hope of Jesus with whoever crosses our path. Let's rededicate our lives to an uncompromising faith and, once again, join the battle!

KNOW HIM BETTER

When a child is born into a family, there is almost an instant bond of love. The parent and child spend LOTS of time together and truly begin to know each other. The parent knows the needs of the child, and the child knows the parent as the provider of comfort and security.

But as the child grows, other activities and friends begin to limit time with parents. In the search for independence, there is often rebellion toward parental instruction and counsel. Soon, the parent and child drift apart and no longer communicate as they once had - they sadly cease to know one another.

Ephesians 1:16-17

"I have not stopped giving thanks for you, remembering you in my prayers. I keep asking that the God of our Lord Jesus Christ, the glorious Father, may give you the Spirit of wisdom and revelation, so that you may know Him better."

Notice this is Paul's continuous prayer; that we be given revelation and wisdom. Revelation is the unveiling of God's truth and wisdom is the application of His truth in our lives. Both of these are necessary and serve the single purpose of knowing Him better.

As we continue in our relationship with Jesus Christ, there is a tendency to hit those Spiritual teenage years where we have things pretty well figured out - or so we think. We begin to gain "self" confidence and trust in our own ability. We get more involved in activities (maybe even "good" activities) and with friends (maybe even "good" friends); but one day we wake and find we've drifted. We didn't intentionally walk away, but there's a definite loss of passion - we no longer really know God.

As a loving father longs to hold his children, our Heavenly Father longs for us to draw near and know Him; "Let him who boasts boast about this: that he understands and knows Me" (Jeremiah 9:24). The Bible always speaks about knowing someone as a very personal and loving relationship: "Adam knew his wife; and she conceived, and bare Cain" (Genesis 4:1 KJV). Jesus even defined eternal life as a state of knowing; "Now this is eternal life: that they may know You, the only true God, and Jesus Christ, whom you have sent" (John 17:3).

The road back to a restored relationship begins with spending time together. No matter how busy we get we must continue to humbly come into the presence of God, confess the sin which causes separation, fellowship with Him in prayer and the quiet study of His Word, and listen intently for His direction. Let's commit (or recommit) to love God with all our heart, soul, mind, and strength; and let's be determined to take the necessary steps to draw near and know Him better.

ALWAYS SEEK HIS COUNSEL

As Moses was about to die, he transferred leadership of Israel to Joshua. God gave His approval of Joshua with the instructions; "Be careful to obey all the law my servant Moses gave you; do not turn from it to the right or to the left, that you may be successful wherever you go" (Joshua 1:7).

Initially, Joshua sought God counsel for every step he took. Joshua received direction for crossing the Jordan river (Joshua 3), building a lasting memorial (Joshua 4), renewing the covenant of circumcision (Joshua 5) and defeating the fortified city of Jericho (Joshua 6). In all of this Joshua listened and obeyed; "So the Lord was with Joshua, and his fame spread throughout the land" (Joshua 6:27).

However, after the miraculous success at Jericho - after Joshua witnessed the city walls fall with the sound of a trumpet and a shout - Joshua's confidence began to grow. When it was time to attack the small city of Ai, Joshua relied on his own strength and the advice of men rather than seeking God.

Joshua 7:3-4

> *"'Send two or three thousand men to take it and do not weary all the people, for only a few men are there.' So about three*

thousand men went up; but they were routed by the men of Ai."

Attacking the city of Ai seemed an insignificant decision. It was a small city and the Israelite army was mighty; and God had already given general instructions to conquer the entire land and an assurance of victory in battle: "I will give you every place where you set your foot...No one will be able to stand up against you" (Joshua 1:3,5). But, unknown to Joshua, there was sin in his camp - spiritual battles which would hinder any physical victory; "That is why the Israelites cannot stand against their enemies" (Joshua 7:12). Our assurance of victory always assumes we are walking with God and in His strength.

When did we last seek and received counsel from God? If it's been longer than the time it took to take our last step, we may be attempting to fight a battle we cannot win. We must never presume to know God's specific plan without asking for specific directions. Just because He said "Go and make disciples of all nations" (Matthew 28:19), doesn't mean we can presume on His method or His timing; "Apart from Me you can do nothing" (John 15:5).

God will show us the way, but we must ask for His guidance; "I have set the Lord always before me. Because He is at my right hand, I will not be shaken" (Psalm 16:8). Our battles are never won because of our strength or the enemy's weakness. They are won only as we allow God to guide our every step. No matter how insignificant the decision may appear, let's be sure to walk in His strength and always seek His counsel.

STAND OUR GROUND

Our Christian walk of growing closer to God and becoming more like His Son involves a process of "renewing our mind" (Romans 12:2). Our mind is renewed as we begin to consider things of eternal value rather than the fading things of the world. But no matter how far we mature in our walk, distractions attempt to consume our thoughts and distance us from God.

These distractions always come in some form of temptation. There's the wide range of self indulging, flesh-filled desires and power hungry ambitions which tempt us at every turn, but there's also the more deceptive temptations like laziness, worry, pride, and overfilled schedules. Each of these are common tools of the enemy used to separate us from an intimate relationship with God. But God is not surprised by temptation - He understands and has provided a way out.

1 Corinthians 10:13

> *"No temptation has seized you except what is common to man. And God is faithful; He will not let you be tempted beyond what you can bear. But when you are tempted, He will also provide a way out so that you can stand up under it."*

In our fight against temptation, we must first understand that being tempted does not mean we've been singled out. Temptations are not an issue of Salvation, and they don't diminish God's love - our temptations are "common to man." Though we don't seem very good at talking about our struggles, we ALL face forms of temptation. We are a Family and have much more in common than we realize.

Since we know we will face temptation as part of our daily battle, let's start our day by getting prepared. No soldier enters war without the proper equipment. Neither should we enter a clearly hostile environment without making sure to get properly dressed; "Therefore put on the full armor of God, so that when the day of evil comes, you may be able to stand your ground" (Ephesians 6:13).

The middle of a tempting situation is not the time to make decisions on how to react. Temptation decisions must be solidified in our heart long before the enemy attempts to pull us off God's path. Conquering temptation is only possible by growing deep roots of commitment and Godly character through daily studying His Word, praying for strength, and trusting in the Holy Spirit to guide our steps - by putting on the "FULL armor of God."

Our Heavenly Father has given us the tools, and He desires for us to live a victorious life. The attacks are going to come (and they will keep coming!) but our way out is to be prepared. If we will begin each day by getting fully dressed for battle, we WILL bear the temptation - we WILL stand our ground.

THE MIND OF CHRIST

In the message "Stand Our Ground" we began with a statement that our Christian walk involves a process of renewing our mind. Paul wrote to the Romans about this renewal as an on-going process of transformation (Romans 12:2). He also wrote about a renewed mind as something which has already occurred; "But we have the mind of Christ" (1 Corinthians 2:16).

This is a consistent message through all the New Testament: through faith in Jesus we are given a new birth, with a new heart, a new Spirit, and a new mind. However, we are continually exhorted to live as a new creation, worship with a new heart, receive guidance and strength from a new Spirit, and make decisions and set priorities with a new mind. We must learn to walk according to the transformed life we have been granted.

Philippians 2:5

"Your attitude (or mind in the KJV) should be the same as that of Christ Jesus."

Many portions of Jesus' life were for the express purpose of giving us an example by which to live. With all the power of the Universe at His command, He humbled Himself and demonstrated the mind and attitude of a servant; "The Son of Man did not come to be served, but to serve" (Matthew 20:28).

He demonstrated a mind of obedience and lived to honor His Father in ALL He did - even though being obedient might result in discomfort or pain...or even death: "My Father, if it is possible, may this cup be taken from Me. Yet not as I will, but as You will" (Matthew 26:39).

As He obediently served, Jesus also demonstrated a mind void of all pride. With more abilities than we can possibly comprehend, Jesus still gave all the glory to His Father; "By Myself I can do nothing...for I seek not to please Myself but Him who sent Me" (John 5:30). His entire life became an example of how we are to be an empty vessel through which God may work.

And even moments before He died - even after being beaten, whipped, spit upon and nailed to a cross - Jesus demonstrated the mind of supreme forgiveness; "Father, forgive them, for they do not know what they are doing" (Luke 23:34).

Though we know we have far to go, the mind of Christ becomes our example. We must develop the mind of a humble servant, void of pride, who desires nothing more than for our Heavenly Father to work in and through our life. We must humbly submit and learn to forgive others as Christ first forgave us. Let's live as His Child. Let's continue to be transformed, and more fully develop the mind of Christ.

SO THE WORLD MAY KNOW

In the message "The Mind of Christ" we considered our call to walk according to the new life we have been given. We then looked at several aspects of Jesus' life as our solid example to follow. We saw His desire to serve and glorify the Father; but probably the most challenging aspect of Jesus' life was His ability to forgive; "Father, forgive them, for they do not know what they are doing" (Luke 23:34).

The walk of a Christian is a life-long process of being transformed into the likeness of Jesus. This process brings us continually closer to God and tangibly shows the gospel message to the world. There is no clearer demonstration of a transformed heart and true love for Christ than when we forgive one another. The simple fact that it's so difficult makes forgiveness a blazing light into a dark and dying world. The unity obtained through forgiveness causes those in the world to be drawn closer to Christ.

John 17:23

"May they be brought to complete unity to let the world know that You sent Me and have loved them even as You have loved Me."

Being united is never a call to compromise the essential truths of the gospel; but it's clearly a call to put aside quarreling over trivial issues and stamp out all jealously, envy, and one of the greatest evils known to man...pride! Pride keeps more people separated from God and more relationships locked in unforgiveness than any other sin.

Continued forgiveness demonstrates the gospel because it requires us to honestly face our pride, place our trust in God, and walk in absolute humility. Forgiveness is not something we can do in our own strength. When we've been "wounded," unfairly treated and misunderstood, our pride wants things to be "even" - demands the other person to confess, repent, and bow to kiss OUR feet. True forgiveness of others brings us back to the cross where we must confess the ugliness of our heart, acknowledge our need for His forgiveness, and, once again, remove ourself from the throne.

Continued forgiveness requires a daily crucifixion of our fleshly, pride-filled self, a submission to the leading of the Holy Spirit, and a complete trust in our Heavenly Father to continue the process He has begun in our life and to fully work in the life of others (according to His perfect timing). This is a life which definitely shines and causes the world to notice.

Let's take a new look at any unforgiveness and determine once and for all to give it to the Lord. Let's glorify our Father and become a living example of the gospel - let's live in unity through love and forgiveness...so the world may know!

THE WATCHMAN

Ezekiel was called to be a prophet after being taken captive to Babylon. Since the beginning of his ministry Ezekiel knew his path would be difficult - he knew the people would not be receptive to his message; "The people to whom I {God} am sending you are obstinate and stubborn" (Ezekiel 2:4). And yet, from the very beginning, God made it clear that Ezekiel was accountable to speak the truth.

Ezekiel 3:17-18

> *"I have made you a watchman; so hear the Word I speak and give them warning from Me. When I say to a wicked man, 'You will surely die,' and you do not warn him...that wicked man will die for his sin, and I will hold you accountable for his blood."*

God called Ezekiel and clearly gave him a message of truth that was expected to be shared; "whether they listen or fail to listen" (Ezekiel 3:11). Ezekiel was not responsible for how many people obediently followed God's Word; but he was definitely accountable for sharing the message God gave.

God's call is not reserved for pastors, missionaries, or ministry leaders. His call goes out to each of us who hear His message of forgiveness. Yes, the world is still full of "obstinate and stubborn" people (we probably need look no further than the mirror); but God's truth is good news which can save lives and give hope - it's a truth which must be shared.

Now here's the difficult part: Sharing God's truth is not an optional part of our walk. Each of us have been called and given a mission field in which to minister; and we are held accountable for our ministry into this field. Notice we're not accountable for the response, only for our action or inaction; "Anyone, then, who knows the good he ought to do and doesn't do it, sins" (James 4:17). Failure to respond to God's leading is sin!

What field has God called you to today? What message has He placed on your heart? There are family, friends, and coworkers who desperately need to hear the gospel message. There are people all around us who need to be encouraged to draw closer to God; encouraged to forgive and restore relationships; encouraged to live according to who they are in Christ. This is our mission field and this is our message! We must obediently share, in love, and under the guidance of the Holy Spirit, even if no one listens.

We are God's watchman over whatever field He provides. Let's draw near and love Him with all our heart - so close to His side that His message and direction are absolutely clear. We must proclaim His truth wherever He leads. Let's accept the responsibility, and accountability, of the watchman.

GIVE HIM ALL THE GLORY

Joseph had some difficult times in his early years. His brothers tried to kill him and then sold him to the Midianites. The Midianites, in turn, sold him as a slave to Potiphar who was one of Pharaoh's officials. Joseph was then falsely accused by Potiphar's wife and thrown in prison where he sat for several years - things definitely weren't going very well.

Then one day Joseph got his opportunity to make a change. Pharaoh had some dreams that bothered him greatly. But when he sent for the wise men of Egypt, no one could help; "Pharaoh told them his dreams, but no one could interpret them for him" (Genesis 41:8). Pharaoh was told of a young Hebrew slave who was in prison, but had demonstrated a unique ability to interpret dreams.

Pharaoh quickly summoned Joseph from the dungeon; "I have heard it said of you that when you hear a dream you can interpret it" (Genesis 41:15). Wow! This was Joseph's big chance - his opportunity to take matters into his own hands and shape his circumstances. He certainly deserved a break. And after all, doesn't God help those who help themselves?

Unfortunately, this is one of the biggest misquotes of the Bible - and a shameful misrepresentation of God. It's much more accurate

33

to say God will faithfully work our circumstances to the good as we diligently seek Him and love Him with all our heart; and faithfully follow where He leads.

Joseph could have used this opportunity to bring glory and honor to himself. But He had learned the important lesson that ALL things come from God and should be used to glorify His name.

Genesis 41:16

"'I cannot do it,' Joseph replied to Pharaoh, 'but God will give Pharaoh the answer he desires.'"

Joseph had been given a wonderful gift, but this gift would only produce fruit as God worked through Joseph's life. This was the same lesson Paul tried to teach the Church in Corinth: "What do you have that you did not receive? And if you did receive it, why do you boast as though you did not?" (1 Corinthians 4:7).

It's by God's grace we accomplish anything; "apart from Me you can do nothing" (John 15:5). It's by His grace we have talents and abilities - it's by His grace we obtain direction and motivation. In fact, it's by His grace we take our next breath! If God provides all the tools, He certainly deserves ALL the praise. Let's never miss an opportunity to use the gifts God has provided. And when our lives produce fruit, let's never miss an opportunity to give Him all the glory!

THE SIN OF ARROGANCE

In the message "Give Him All The Glory" we considered how Joseph recognized his ability to interpret dreams was only by God's grace; "God will give Pharaoh the answer he desires" (Genesis 41:16). We were also reminded of Paul's words to the Corinthians, "What do you have that you did not receive?" (1 Corinthians 4:7), and of the words of Jesus, "apart from Me you can do nothing" (John 15:5). Giving all glory to God reflects an understanding of who we are in Christ and, more importantly, who He is in us!

As we see the multitude of sin in the world today, which cause others such pain, we must be reminded that all sin can be traced to pride and a lack of humility - to arrogance, a self-exaltation where we think of ourself and our abilities more highly than we should; and, in the end, attempt to elevate ourself above God.

James wrote about this arrogance when he said, "do not slander one another" (James 4:11). He said when we are unfairly critical of others we not only disobey God's law of love, but we are actually speaking against God's law and sitting in judgment over the law - and there is only one Judge! (James 4:11-12). Willful disobedience involves elevating ourself to the throne of

God and judging which of His truths apply to our life. This is the ultimate arrogance!

Isaiah 14:13-15

"You said in your heart, 'I will ascend to heaven; I will raise my throne above the stars of God; I will sit enthroned on the mount of assembly, on the utmost heights of the sacred mountain. I will ascend above the tops of the clouds; I will make myself like the Most High.' But you are brought down to the grave, to the depths of the pit."

This passage may be referring to Satan, or an earthly king in the time of Isaiah. Either way, it clearly details the true heart of pride as well as the end result for such a heart. Isaiah is warning us all about the danger of attempting to raise ourself to the level of God. After all, this temptation is what caused the fall of all mankind in the Garden of Eden; "when you eat of it your eyes will be opened, and you will be like God" (Genesis 3:5).

We must continue to examine our heart and aggressively cut away all areas of pride before they infect and contaminate our whole being. Can we ever rid ourself of all pride? Can we ever cease all sin? I don't believe we can! But I know that on the day we see Him face to face, we will be fully transformed, fully glorified, and fully able to praise Him for all eternity. Until the day He calls us home, we must continually say, "He must become greater, I must become less" (John 3:30). Until that day, we must diligently battle the sin of arrogance.

A GOD OF CONVENIENCE

Paul had been arrested and sent to Caesarea to stand trial before Governor Felix. During Paul's trial, he spoke of his worship of God and belief in His Word. Felix kept Paul in prison, but often talked with him about his faith.

Acts 24:24-25

> *"He sent for Paul and listened to him as he spoke about faith in Christ Jesus. As Paul discoursed on righteousness, self-control and the judgment to come, Felix was afraid and said, 'That's enough for now! You may leave. When I find it convenient, I will send for you.'"*

Governor Felix had the ability to hear the gospel from the greatest theologian of all time and yet failed to act on what he heard.

Several years earlier, Herod had arrested John the Baptist for speaking against his marriage (Herod was married to his own brother's wife). Though Herod wanted to kill John, he also feared and respected him because he was a righteous and holy man: "When Herod heard John, he was greatly puzzled; yet he liked to listen to him" (Mark 6:20). Herod liked to listen to John's uncompromising message of repentance, and yet he failed to act on what he heard.

37

When Jesus was arrested, Pilate came face to face with the Son of God. He heard Jesus calmly claim to be King of the Jews and to have special favor from God; "You would have no power over Me if it were not given to you from above" (John 19:11). Pilate listened to Jesus, found no fault, and tried to set Him free (John 19:12) - but in the end, Pilate failed to act on the truth.

Most of us experience a wonderful religious freedom today. We have free access to God's Word and can usually find a local church willing to preach the truth. Yet, how often do we fail to act on what we receive? How often do our religious activities become cold and mechanical, lacking any real interest? "These people come near to Me with their mouth and honor Me with their lips, but their hearts are far from Me" (Isaiah 29:13).

If our worship does not invade every area of our life, then God is not on the throne. We must trust Him in ALL things! We must have a passion for His Word as well as an uncompromising willingness to act. We must long for His presence each and every day - not just during our once a week worship.

Let's NEVER put God on the shelf or ask Him to be "on-call." He's the Creator of the Universe who has called us to a life of full time worship. Let's never treat our Heavenly Father as a God of convenience.

HEART FULL OF PASSION

In the message "A God of Convenience" we were encouraged to be true worshipers who walk with God every day and refuse to put Him "on the shelf." We must never become people who worship with our lips, but have hearts which are far from God (Isaiah 29:13). We must be careful not to stray from the path of devoted love to become entangled in the weeds and thorns of selfish convenience.

But how can we guard against such wandering? How can we recognize when we are beginning to stray? And how can we return to the place we truly desire?

The answer to these questions will always be found in a deep and passionate love! Our relationship with God is not based on an exercise of our intellect, it is based on a transformation of our heart. Our relationship began with a work of the Spirit as our heart became His. It must now continue as we walk so close that our only desire is to give Him ALL our heart - to give Him what is already His.

After years of successful rule, David's kingdom was now in total rebellion. His son, Absalom, was attempting to become the new king and had forced David to flee into the desert. With his life's work falling apart, and far from his home and place of worship, David turned to God and gave us a clear picture of Godly passion.

Psalm 63:1-4

"O God, You are my God, earnestly I seek You; my soul thirsts for You, my body longs for You, in a dry and weary land where there is no water. I have seen You in the sanctuary and beheld Your power and Your glory. Because Your love is better than life, my lips will glorify You. I will praise You as long as I live, and in Your name I will lift up my hands."

Although it may be difficult to maintain this level of passion every moment of the day, this IS the relationship to which we have been called. This is worship! We must realize that this world is a "dry and weary land" when compared to walking in His presence. We must long for God's love more than life itself and seek to glorify Him in all we do.

If this type of relationship sounds foreign - maybe even a little radical - then I invite you to "taste and see that the Lord is good" (Psalm 34:8). He will pour out His blessings on those who step out in faith and truly give Him their heart. If you already understand this relationship but realize the passion has faded, then I boldly exhort you to return. Return to what you know will truly satisfy - to what you know is eternal, imperishable. Let's all return to the place of true worship. Let's all draw near and worship with a heart full of passion.

REMEMBER THE ETERNAL

Heavenly Father, we pray for comfort and peace for those directly affected by the tragic events this week. For those who lost loved ones, we pray that You would become their refuge and source of strength. For the children who lost a parent, we pray their hearts would remain tender and receptive to Your Word. We pray for those searching for answers. Please reveal Your truth and help us all to understand that apart from You, there is nothing! In Jesus Name we pray, Amen.

This prayer was written after the tragedy with the Space Shuttle on February 1, 2003. But a similar prayer was distributed after September 11, 2001 because of the World Trade Center tragedy. And unfortunately, it could also be a prayer for every day of the year because of the thousands who die in automobile accidents, or as a result of senseless violence or disease; or those whose life ends because of starvation or addiction to drugs. These lives seem needlessly shortened, but even life which reaches its "full-potential" is incredibly short; "What is your life? You are a mist that appears for a little while and then vanishes" (James 4:14).

When tragedy occurs we ought to sincerely pray for those affected; it's not often the whole world can pray for a specific group of people.

41

But we also should take a moment to consider the frailty and brevity of life, and how our priorities reflect this truth. We must strive for a firmer understanding that anything outside the will of God will one day fade away. Any other "god" who receives our worship in the form of excess time, thought, energy, or resources will most surely burn and be swept aside.

1 Corinthians 7:29,31

"What I mean, brothers, is that the time is short. From now on...those who use the things of the world, {use them} as if not engrossed in them. For this world in its present form is passing away."

No matter how many times I read these truths of God's Word, I know I don't yet fully understand. I know our time is short, but I continually gain my identity and become engrossed in my toys. Father forgive me!

If there is any good to come out of tragedy, it will only be as we resolve to "fix our eyes not on what is seen, but on what is unseen" (2 Corinthians 4:18a). We must allow events such as these to firmly establish that "what is seen is temporary, but what is unseen is eternal" (2 Corinthians 4:18b).

It's time we turn our heart to God in true revival and do ALL as unto the Lord. We can no longer give our lives to what is temporary and passing away. It's time we unashamedly worship Him and follow where He leads. It's time we draw close to His presence and remember the eternal.

WHAT THE LORD HAS PROVIDED

As a young teenage boy, David showed a deep understanding of God's strength as he prepared to fight Goliath; "The Lord who delivered me from the paw of the lion and the paw of the bear will deliver me from the hand of this Philistine" (1 Samuel 17:37). The understanding that God was fighting the battle allowed David to confidently approach Goliath with nothing more than a sling and a few stones; "This day the Lord will hand you over to me" (1 Samuel 17:46).

After many years of being pursued by king Saul, David demonstrated his belief that every victory he enjoyed came as a direct result of God's hand.

The Amalekites had raided the village where David and his men were living. Under God's promise of victory, David set off with six hundred men to battle the enemy and take back their stolen possessions; but two hundred of the men were too tired to join the fight. After the victorious battle, the four hundred who fought wanted to exclude the two hundred who stayed behind; "Because they did not go out with us, we will not share with them the plunder we recovered" (1 Samuel 30:22). But David reminded them Who really won the battle.

1 Samuel 30:23

"No, my brothers, you must not do that with what the Lord has given us. He has protected us and handed over to us the forces that came against us."

David understood it wouldn't have mattered whether four hundred or forty, or even four, had gone into battle - it wouldn't have mattered whether the men were skilled or unskilled - the battle would have been won. The battle was won because of God's promise and His provision, not because of the men's ability.

As we see the battle approaching we must draw even closer to our Heavenly Father. He has given us abilities which we must use, but then we must place all our trust in Him for the results. If the battle appears to be a failure, we must trust that God is in control and working toward His good and perfect plan. When God is in control, there are no failures as viewed through His eyes. And if the battle appears to be victorious, we must not allow our pride to take credit for the work God has done - for this always results in failure, regardless of our view.

God owns ALL and provides ALL. He owns our possessions, our relationships, and our ministries. He owns our abilities as well as our lack - our successes as well as our failures. As we come through our next battle (and we will!) - in fact, even in the midst of the battle - let's return the ownership and give Him all the glory. We must never attempt to control or hold tight to that which the Lord has provided.

OUR SPIRITUAL WALLS

Nehemiah lived in the days following Jerusalem's captivity in Babylon. The first captives had been allowed to return to Jerusalem and reconstruct the temple. However, those who returned had left the walls of the city in great disrepair. When Nehemiah heard this discouraging report, he asked permission of the king to return to Jerusalem and rebuild the once mighty walls.

Nehemiah's request was granted. He traveled to Jerusalem in the year 445 BC and motivated the people to rebuild the walls in record time. But Nehemiah discovered there was more broken in Jerusalem than just physical walls. It had been many years since the people truly worshipped God - Spiritual walls were now in desperate need of mending.

Nehemiah knew the only way toward Spiritual repair was through the Word of God. He gathered the people, and they wept as Ezra read God's Word "from daybreak till noon" (Nehemiah 8:3). For seven days, Ezra continued to read from God's Word. On the eighth day, walls began to mend as the people "spent another quarter {of the day} in confession and worshipping the Lord" (Nehemiah 9:3). True repair occurred as they recommitted their lives to following the commands of God.

45

Nehemiah 10:29

"All these now bind themselves with a curse and an oath to follow the Law of God given through Moses...and to obey carefully all the commands, regulations and decrees of the Lord."

Our world continues to change. Nations continue to build physical walls and attack one another, but show little concern for the Spiritual walls which protect from the real enemy. Years of neglect, and large scale drifting from God's path, have left our Spiritual walls cracked and vulnerable. Our families are seldom led by God and our courts make laws without seeking His counsel. Attacks come from every direction and our defenses are weak!

The repair of our Spiritual walls will not occur at the national level. Governments have become too large and diverse to even recognize this need. But we have the opportunity all around the world to rebuild one individual, one family, one church, and one community at a time. We have the ability to repair the portion of wall within our circle of influence. Together, we CAN rebuild and strengthen!!

As in the time of Nehemiah, we must return to a passion for the Word of God. His Word reveals His plan through faith in His Son, and guidance and strength through His Spirit. Let's become people dedicated to study and prayer, and allow each day of our lives to be led by God's Spirit. Let's make a lasting commitment to focus on the eternal and rebuild our Spiritual walls.

THE TRUE PEACE OF GOD

Each of us is striving toward the "success-ful" life, though our definitions of success may often differ. Many of us place our effort in obtaining more and better things, reaching a higher status, or building greater security; others, involve themselves in more "spiritual" endeavors with ministry activities and service projects. But the root motivation for all our effort is the same: we all are seeking a life full of peace.

Unfortunately, the world trains us to simply set and then exceed our goals without ever taking the time to examine what our heart really longs for - we all are striving for peace! I'm certainly not opposed to goals; but we must understand that meeting every single goal, by itself, will NEVER result in peace.

The lack of peace is, first and foremost, the result of our sinful condition. When Adam and Eve chose to place their will ahead of God's by eating the forbidden fruit, sin entered the world and true peace became illusive; "when you eat of it you will surely die" (Genesis 2:17). We will never obtain true peace through different governments; nor will we ever be able to pur-chase our peace or create peace by changing our surroundings. Peace begins with the for-giveness of sin through faith in Jesus and grows as we live in submission to the Holy Spirit; "The mind of sinful man is death, but the mind controlled by the Spirit is life and peace" (Romans 8:6).

In Paul's letter to the Philippians, he said those who have placed their faith in Jesus now have a basic formula for a life of peace.

Philippians 4:4-7

"Rejoice in the Lord always. I will say it again: Rejoice! Let your gentleness be evident to all. The Lord is near. Do not be anxious about anything, but in everything, by prayer and petition, with thanksgiving, present your requests to God. And the peace of God, which transcends all understanding, will guard your hearts and your minds in Christ Jesus."

Our formula for peace is: 1) Rejoice, 2) Rejoice some more, 3) Be gentle, 4) Know God is near, 5) Remove all anxiety, and 6) Pray about everything with a thankful heart. Jesus promised that those who trust in Him will receive a peace beyond anything this world can understand: "Peace I leave with you; My peace I give you. I do not give to you as the world gives. Do not let your hearts be troubled and do not be afraid" (John 14:27).

If our lives are lacking peace, the ONLY solution is to draw nearer to God, trust Him more, and rejoice (and rejoice and rejoice) as we are guided by His Spirit. Only then will we find the "success" we have been striving for - only then will we obtain what our heart longs for...the true peace of God!

THE MOST HOLY PLACE

One of the amazingly consistent themes through all of God's Word is His desire to fellowship with His children. When God created Adam and placed him in the Garden of Eden, Adam was allowed to enjoy God's presence. God brought Adam the animals to name (Genesis 2:19) and actually walked with Adam during the day. However, this fellowship was broken and man was cast out of God's presence when Adam sinned by eating the forbidden fruit.

Many years later, God formed the nation of Israel to be a people fully devoted to Him. When God led the Israelites out of Egyptian slavery, He told Moses to construct a holy place for His presence to reside. God called this the Most Holy Place and instructed it be separated from the rest of the tabernacle by a curtain.

Leviticus 16:2

"The Lord said to Moses: 'Tell your brother Aaron not to come whenever he chooses into the Most Holy Place behind the curtain in front of the atonement cover on the ark, or else he will die, because I appear in the cloud over the atonement cover.'"

The presence of God resided in the Most Holy Place, behind a curtain, and could only be entered by the High Priest once a year on the Day of Atonement. The High Priest would enter the Most Holy Place with the blood of a goat as a sacrifice for the sins of the people (Leviticus 16:15).

God loved us so much, and so greatly desires a lasting and intimate fellowship, that He gave His Son to be the final sacrifice for our sins: "He did not enter by means of the blood of goats and calves; but He entered the Most Holy Place once for all by His own blood, having obtained eternal redemption" (Hebrews 9:12).

When Jesus died on the cross, "the curtain of the temple was torn in two from top to bottom" (Matthew 27:51). His sacrifice provides a way for us to enter into the presence of God at any moment; "We have confidence to enter the Most Holy Place by the blood of Jesus" (Hebrews 10:19).

God is calling us to reach out and draw near to His presence through faith in the sacrifice of His Son. The Creator of the Universe is knocking at the door; "If anyone hears My voice and opens the door, I will come in and eat with him, and he with Me" (Revelation 3:20). Our Heavenly Father is calling us to an eternity of fellowship. Let's open the door and enter His presence today - let's enter the Most Holy Place.

HIS GENTLE KNOCK

In the message "The Most Holy Place" we saw how Jesus became the final sacrifice for our sin. When Jesus died on the cross, "the curtain of the temple was torn in two from top to bottom" (Matthew 27:51). The curtain had, up to that point, formed a barrier for the Most Holy Place in the temple where God resided with His people. The tearing of the curtain was a clear demonstration that anyone who believes in Jesus for the forgiveness of sin can now enter the presence of God; "We have confidence to enter the Most Holy Place by the blood of Jesus" (Hebrews 10:19).

We are a fortunate people! Not since Adam has man had such access to the presence of God. We no longer need a priest with a specific sacrifice, and we need not pray a specific prayer - but there IS a condition. The Most Holy Place of the presence of God can only be entered by those who come by faith in Jesus Christ. If we desire the presence of God, we must first open the door of our heart.

Revelation 3:20

"Here I am! I stand at the door and knock. If anyone hears My voice and opens the door, I will come in and eat with him, and he with Me."

51

Here is contained the great mystery of God's plan for man - He desires a people who recognize their need, hear His voice, and open the door to invite Him in. He then promises to enter and "set His seal of ownership on us, and put His Spirit in our hearts as a deposit, guaranteeing what is to come" (2 Corinthians 1:22).

God's Word never indicates that Jesus will crash through the door of our heart; He's never pictured as huffing and puffing to blow the door down. And He certainly NEVER sneaks in through a side window! He simply and patiently stands at the door and knocks - He says, "I am here. Won't you invite Me in?"

Opening the door involves an understanding of who Jesus is, and an act of submission which releases control of our life. We may hear His voice through something someone says or something we read - we may "hear" Him knocking as we sit in silence - but when we hear, we must be willing to open the door; "Today, if you hear His voice, do not harden your hearts" (Hebrews 3:15).

Many people will hear the knock of Jesus, but few will open the door. Most will spend a lifetime evaluating the knock and analyzing the One who is knocking; some will even push a little food onto the front porch; but few will actually recognize their need and open the door. Let's invite Him in today and commune with Him EVERY day for all eternity. Today, let's answer His gentle knock.

HIS DISCIPLES

One of the last commands Jesus gave was to "go and make disciples of all nations" (Matthew 28:19). The making of a disciple is the complete work of the Holy Spirit; but we are told to join in this work by teaching people to believe in the sacrifice of Jesus for the forgiveness of sin, to humbly submit control of their life into His hands, and to "obey everything I have commanded you" (Matthew 28:20).

God's Word contains the complete description of what it means to believe, submit, and obey. Jesus taught extensively on each of these issues. But the single command which will have the greatest impact on the world around us is the command to love.

John 13:34-35

"A new command I give you: Love one another. As I have loved you, so you must love one another. By this all men will know that you are My disciples, if you love one another."

The phrase "As I have loved you" ought to rip at our heart. Though there was nothing in us to deserve His love, Jesus gave His life. And long before He gave His physical life, He laid down the very essence of who He was; "but

53

made Himself nothing, taking the very nature of a servant, being made in human likeness" (Philippians 2:7). Jesus loved enough to give up who He was for those completely unlovable; and this is the level of love we are called to demonstrate to one another.

We are called to a sacrificial love - a love that gives and considers others needs ahead of our own. We are called to give our time, our tears, our understanding, and even our material resources when necessary. We are called to love enough to rejoice when others rejoice, but also to hurt when others hurt; and to forgive simply because Jesus first forgave us. We are called to love!

But notice why we are called to such love. Our love for others is certainly an expression of gratitude to God and a maturing process as we grow into the likeness of Christ; but Jesus also says our love for others is the one sure way of telling the world we are followers of Christ. Our love becomes an act of worship because, through love, we are boldly declaring: Jesus is Lord! As we love - even when others may not "deserve" our love - we actively show the world the joy and peace found only in Jesus.

The world is overflowing with people who need love - who have run out of hope, longing for someone to let them know they care. We are those who must care! We must reach out to one another with a love that defies all worldly wisdom and understanding. We must love as Jesus loved us. This love will be used to work miracles; this love will bring glory and honor to our Heavenly Father; this love will show the world that we are truly His disciples.

UNITED IN PURPOSE

In the message "His Disciples" we saw how our love for one another demonstrates we are true followers of Jesus Christ; "By this all men will know that you are My disciples, if you love one another" (John 13:35). We saw our call for a sacrificial love, and focused on those with clear needs - the lonely, hurting, anxious, depressed or hungry - needs which require definite action.

But there's another expression of Christian love - a love which is still sacrificial, but one that requires us to withhold certain actions, place restraints on our words, and definitely increase our time in prayer. This is the love which leads to unity in our local fellowship.

1 Corinthians 1:10

"I appeal to you, brothers, in the name of our Lord Jesus Christ, that all of you agree with one another so there may be no divisions among you and that you may be perfectly united in mind and thought."

There's a story of a man lost at sea. He's treading water and has given up all hope. Suddenly, a ship appears on the horizon and moves his way. His strength surges as he wildly waves his arms, rescue is near! But as the ship gets closer, he sees the passengers yelling at one another; many are punching, kicking and spitting; and some are even being thrown overboard. It doesn't take long for the man to begin swimming as fast as he can AWAY from the ship.

We are passengers on the gospel ship, and God's Word continually calls us to unity; "conduct yourself in a manner worthy of the gospel of Christ...stand firm in one spirit, contending as one man for the faith of the gospel" (Philippians 1:27). If we are united with Christ, we ought to be "like-minded, having the same love, being one in spirit and purpose" (Philippians 2:2). As Jesus prayed to the Father, He made it clear why we are to unite: "so the world may believe that You have sent Me" (John 17:21).

Unity is never a call for compromise on the essentials of the gospel. We must never give a single step of ground regarding the necessity and sufficiency of total surrender to Jesus. But when we begin to divide over issues like the format of our worship service, the structure of our programs, or the look of our facility, we have clearly stepped over the line of Biblical unity.

I can't define the exact line of unity in your local fellowship. But I can confidently suggest there is greater room for unity than what first appears. If all of us will honestly remove our pride and understand God's purpose in a unified fellowship, we will see much more room for grace and love. Let's truly show the love of Christ. Let's all draw closer and closer to Jesus and show the world we are united in Spirit, united in purpose.

WE WILL NOT FEAR

In these times of great uncertainty - with concerns about war, terrorism, and the economy - let's always remember, our Heavenly Father is the Creator of the Universe. He formed the Heavens and the Earth out of nothing, and as we place our trust in Him, He has given a basic promise: "Never will I leave you, never will I forsake you" (Hebrews 13:5). His desire is for us to draw nearer in our love and worship, and allow His Spirit to remove all fear.

Psalm 46:1-3

"God is our refuge and strength, an ever-present help in trouble. Therefore we will not fear, though the earth give way and the mountains fall into the heart of the sea, though its waters roar and foam and the mountains quake with their surging."

Although we are uncertain what tomorrow may bring, we ought to have confidence in the One who really controls tomorrow. If we believe Jesus died for our sin, rose again in victory over death, and is seated at the right hand of the Father - if we surrender our life to who He is and what He has done - our eternal home has been firmly established; "Our citizenship is in Heaven" (Philippians 3:20). As a child of the Sovereign King - as one who believes in our eternal future - we no longer have reason to fear; "For you did not receive a spirit that makes you a slave again to fear, but you received the Spirit of sonship" (Romans 8:15).

We no longer have a reason, but still we fear. The unknown is scary and makes us feel out of control. But as we pray for an end to violence - as we strive to make this world safer, better educated, and more prosperous - we must understand there is only one true solution to our fear.

Our fear will only be removed as we love the Lord with ALL our heart, soul, mind and strength. When we understand that our life is not our own, we will love with a complete abandonment to His desire. We will pray and live each day with the surrender demonstrated by Christ; "Father...not My will, but Yours be done" (Luke 22:42). As we live each day to bring Him glory and honor, fear WILL be removed: "There is no fear in love. But perfect love drives out fear" (1 John 4:18).

Yes, these days contain some uncertainty. If we continue to focus on what we can see, there will always be uncertainties. But our faith, hope, and joy are in His eternal glory - not in this world which will one day pass away. Let's refuse to allow our fear of the unknown cripple our service for God. There is still much work He has for us to do. Let's pray that our love will increase, that our worship will intensify, and that we will boldly stand up and proclaim: "We will not fear!"

JUST PASSING THROUGH

It's a great privilege to be part of God's creation. It's an honor to view "God's invisible qualities - His eternal power and divine nature" (Romans 1:20) - through the beauty of this world. Every plant and animal; every hill, valley and body of water; every star in the sky and every man, woman and child declare the glory of God and attest to His majesty. And yet, as glorious as this world may be...it is not our home.

Philippians 3:19-21

"Their mind is on earthly things. But our citizenship is in Heaven. And we eagerly await a Savior from there, the Lord Jesus Christ, who, by the power that enables Him to bring everything under His control, will transform our lowly bodies so that they will be like His glorious body."

When we place our trust in Jesus, He provides a way for us to be united with God and "adopted as His sons" (Ephesians 1:5). We are adopted by grace and become "fellow citizens with God's people and members of God's household" (Ephesians 2:19). If we could gain even a small understanding of "God's household," we would hold very loose any of our attachments to this world.

Abraham lived his life by faith. When God called Abraham to pack all his household and move, he obeyed "even though he did not know where he was going" (Hebrews 11:8). Abraham was never concerned with his earthly dwelling; he was "longing for a better country - a Heavenly one" (Hebrews 11:16). Abraham honored God through faith while remaining an "alien and a stranger on earth" (Hebrews 11:13).

We have been placed in this world with all its beauty and with all its temptations. In fact, when we give our life to Christ, we are specifically sent into the world for the purpose of ministry; "As You have sent Me into the world, I have sent them into the world" (John 17:18). But we must NEVER become identified by the values of the world nor driven by anything it can offer. We are sent into the world, but we must never be of the world; "They are not of the world, even as I am not of it" (John 17:16).

Our home is defined as the place we feel most comfortable; the place we store our treasures and find rest for our soul. If we are a child of God, our eternal home is Heaven and we ought to be able to say, "Take everything I own but leave me Jesus and I will have enough!" This world can be VERY beautiful and our lives should always be a productive expression of worship for our Lord. But let's always remember...we're just passing through!

IN WHOM WE TRUST

Hezekiah became the king of Judah soon after the northern tribes of Israel had been taken captive by the Assyrians. Judah was now being threatened by this same Assyrian army. Hezekiah was young and had a strong desire to do right in the eyes of God, but his faith was being greatly tested.

Seeing his kingdom would soon be under attack, Hezekiah sought help through an alliance with Egypt. Though this alliance was not wrong in itself, the action was taken out of fear and without consulting God. This action was not only foolish, it was sin!

Isaiah 31:1

> *"Woe to those who go down to Egypt for help, who rely on horses, who trust in the multitude of their chariots and in the great strength of their horsemen, but do not look to the Holy One of Israel, or seek help from the Lord."*

Hezekiah made the same mistake all too common among believers today. We say we believe God's Word is true, but fail to trust Him with the real trials of our life. It was easier for Hezekiah to place his trust in what he could see, than in the Hand of God which he "believed" but remained unseen.

When the Assyrians actually attacked Jerusalem, Hezekiah's faith had greatly increased. As he spoke with his soldiers, Hezekiah demonstrated full confidence in God.

2 Chronicles 32:7-8

"Do not be afraid or discouraged because of the king of Assyria and the vast army with him, for there is a greater power with us than with him. With him is only the arm of flesh, but with us is the Lord our God to help us and to fight our battles."

Where do we turn when the enemy threatens? If our faith is restricted to the inside of church walls on Sunday morning, we are definitely ill-prepared. We must learn to walk in the presence of God all through our day so we KNOW God is with us.

When we trust Him and love Him with ALL our heart, we begin to walk in victory regardless of the physical outcome of a particular battle. God may certainly direct us to protect ourselves, or avoid conflict; but with our eyes firmly set on Jesus, we must understand the real war has already been won. This is simply worth repeating: regardless of the outcome in each of life's many battles, the end of the Book has already been written...Jesus wins! When we are under attack, let's put substance to our faith and allow our lives to demonstrate in Whom we trust!

THE MOST IMPORTANT QUESTION

We seem to spend an enormous amount of time evaluating questions about our future: what school we'll attend, what job we will work, who we will marry, and where we will live. These are important questions and deserve careful consideration. But have we given proper thought to the question which determines our eternal future?

If the Bible is simply a collection of stories and the thoughts of crazy men, then there is no eternity and you need read no further - the next several years are all we have, so make the most of them. But if the Bible is God's direct message, then there is nothing of greater importance! His message says we continue to live long after our physical body ceases to breathe. Though we pass from this earth, we continue to live - we either live in eternal joy and peace, or eternal pain and suffering. There is no greater question: Where WILL we spend eternity?

When Jesus died, He was nailed to a cross along with two other men. These men were thieves and both mocked Jesus for claiming to be the Son of God. But at some point during those long hours on the cross, one of the men demonstrated a changed heart and had his eternal future radically altered.

Luke 23:40-41

"'Don't you fear God,' he said, 'since you are under the same sentence? We are punished justly, for we are getting what our deeds deserve. But this man has done nothing wrong.'"

In the last moment of life, this common thief pointed the way to eternal peace. He recognized his sin and understood he deserved death. We ALL sin and fall short of God's standard; and this sin deserves death, eternal pain and suffering. But praise God we need not dwell in this hopeless state. The thief turned from his sin, toward Jesus as the One who would conquer death; "Jesus, remember me when You come into Your Kingdom" (Luke 23:42).

Though the thief had nothing to give, he surrendered ALL. God's Word never says there are specific acts which determine our eternal future. We are simply told to believe in Jesus with such a belief that we call out with complete surrender. When the thief recognized and turned from his sin, with humility toward Jesus as his only hope, Jesus answered as He promises to answer us today; "I tell you the truth, today you will be with Me in paradise" (Luke 23:43).

In that moment the thief had his answer. No longer a thief but a Child of God, he would live forever in joy and peace. Let's not allow another day to go by without knowing where we will spend eternity! Have we recognized and turned from the sin within our heart? Have we humbly placed our life in His hands? Do we really believe? Today, let's make sure we know the answer to the most important question.

LET IT SHINE

After walking with His disciples for three years, Jesus gave the command to "go and make disciples of all nations" (Matthew 28:19). Jesus taught them the full gospel message and revealed the wonderful truths about our Heavenly Father: "I have made You known to them and will continue to make You known" (John 17:26).

The disciples had been blessed with an awesome knowledge of the truth and now had the responsibility to take this message to all the nations; "teaching them to obey everything I have commanded you" (Matthew 28:19-20). This was not a new command. Toward the beginning of Jesus' ministry, He taught about the need to share our life in Christ with others.

Matthew 5:14-16

"You are the light of the world. A city on a hill cannot be hidden. Neither do people light a lamp and put it under a bowl. Instead they put it on a stand, and it gives light to everyone in the house. In the same way, let your light shine before men."

When we place our faith in Jesus for the forgiveness of sin we are "rescued from the dominion of darkness" (Colossians 1:13).

Where darkness once ruled, the Light of Jesus now reigns supreme: "Whoever follows Me will never walk in darkness, but will have the Light of life" (John 8:12). Receiving His free gift of light allows us to see His path and also lights the path for others to follow!

Being given the Light of Christ is an awesome blessing, but with this gift also comes a very real responsibility. Every day God gives us opportunities to share our faith, to share our light; but when we keep silent, we cover our lamp and deprive our flame of vital oxygen. It doesn't take long for such a flame to begin to weaken, flicker, and die!

We must keep the fire going by sharing our faith! As a child of God, we have become "Christ's ambassadors, as though God were making His appeal through us" (2 Corinthians 5:20). Though God doesn't need us to accomplish His work, He has invited (even commanded) us to play a part in His wonderful plan. The world was Spiritually dark when Jesus arrived and there remains many areas of darkness today. But we have the responsibility, and the privilege, of helping to light one small corner.

Let's faithfully share the truth of Jesus wherever we are sent. When we receive the Light of Christ, we should no more keep it to ourselves than we should keep our breath inside our body once we are born (neither are very healthy). This precious gift, given by grace through faith, comes with a command. We must continue to hold the Light high and let it shine!

COMPELLED TO MINISTER

In the message "Let It Shine" we considered our responsibility to shine the light of Jesus into the world. God will sometimes use powerful preachers to share the gospel message with thousands; but most often, He uses common people like you and me to share His love with one individual at a time.

But for most, sharing the gospel doesn't come naturally. We fear offending, fear rejection, and mostly we fear not having the right answers. A portion of these fears are perfectly natural. But our fears are always magnified by the enemy who seeks to keep us silent. Satan hates for us to speak the truth!

God chose Jeremiah to be a prophet forty years prior to Israel's captivity in Babylon. This was a difficult time to be God's spokesman - His message was not at all pleasant. From his first days as a prophet, Jeremiah was told to speak of approaching doom; "From the north disaster will be poured out on all who live in the land" (Jeremiah 1:14). God was going to discipline the nation for their many years of sinful rebellion and Jeremiah was sent to warn and explain why.

Jeremiah had his share of fear about sharing God's message; "Ah, Sovereign Lord, I do not know how to speak; I am only a child"

(Jeremiah 1:6). His words certainly match some of ours today. But Jeremiah was obedient and placed his trust in God's promise; "Do not be afraid of them, for I am with you and will rescue you" (Jeremiah 1:8).

After many years of proclaiming God's message, Jeremiah's life had become nearly unbearable. Nobody believed his message and, instead of repenting, the people mocked and ridiculed; "The Word of the Lord has brought me insult and reproach all day long" (Jeremiah 20:8). Jeremiah had every reason to walk away from his calling, but something wonderful had taken root in his heart.

Jeremiah 20:9

"If I say, 'I will not mention Him or speak any more in His name,' His Word is in my heart like a fire, a fire shut up in my bones. I am weary of holding it in; indeed, I cannot."

For many years, Jeremiah had pressed close to God - seeking His direction and desiring to do His will. Jeremiah knew the presence of God and could not conceive of life apart from His Lord. Despite great hardship, he could no longer imagine his life void of ministering and proclaiming God's Truth!

His Word is never a burden too heavy to carry. But we will continue to struggle until we draw close and fill our lives with His presence. When we can see nothing but His majesty and glory, His Word will no longer be contained. Only then will we truly shine. Only then will we be compelled to minister.

LEAVE EVERYTHING AND FOLLOW

When Jesus walked on the earth, He called a few select people to follow Him as He ministered. There was something irresistible about His call - something that opened eyes to a new reality and caused a radical change.

Luke 9:23-25

"If anyone would come after Me, he must deny himself and take up his cross daily and follow Me. For whoever wants to save his life will lose it, but whoever loses his life for Me will save it. What good is it for a man to gain the whole world, and yet lose or forfeit his very self?"

Peter, James and John were partners in a small fishing business on the Sea of Galilee. This was their source of support for themselves as well as their families. Yet when they heard the call to become "fishers of men," they eagerly responded; "So they pulled their boats up on shore, left everything and followed Him" (Luke 5:11).

Matthew (also called Levi) was a tax collector - a Jew appointed by the Roman government to collect taxes from his Jewish brothers. As a tax collector, Matthew made a good living; but he walked away from his life of security when

Jesus called: "'Follow Me,' Jesus said to him, and Levi got up, left everything and followed Him" (Luke 5:27-28).

In the Old Testament, Abraham moved his entire household to follow God without even knowing where he was being sent (Genesis 12:1-5). Moses, at eighty years old, left the peaceful life of tending flocks to follow God's call to confront Pharaoh (Exodus 3). And Elisha completely destroyed his old way of life when Elijah called: "He took his yoke of oxen and slaughtered them. He burned the plowing equipment to cook the meat and gave it to the people. Then he set out to follow Elijah" (1 Kings 19:21).

Answering the call to follow will always require a change; but the change may not be in physical location, profession, or status. King Solomon followed God and was the richest man on earth. Joseph followed God and was the second most powerful man in Egypt. There will always be a change as we take up our cross to follow, but the change is in our heart. It's a change where we learn "the secret of being content...whether well fed or hungry, whether living in plenty or in want" (Philippians 4:12). It's a change where we leave our old values and priorities, and find complete fulfillment in following Jesus.

As we draw closer to our Heavenly Father, we will find His call to be irresistible. We will learn the freedom and power of daily being led by His Spirit. And, as with the Saints of old, we will NEVER regret answering the call to leave everything and follow.

INTO THE STORM

Immediately after feeding five thousand men, plus women and children, with five loaves of bread and two fish, "Jesus made the disciples get into the boat and go on ahead of Him to the other side" (Matthew 14:22). The disciples began to cross the Sea of Galilee when a storm arose which caused them to "strain against the oars" (Mark 6:48). It was the middle of the night and after already rowing about three and a half miles they found themselves fighting against the wind and waves.

Why had this happened? The disciples had done exactly what Jesus told them to do and now they were facing a major struggle. They had clearly heard and obeyed; but they were still confronting a very difficult situation. The story continued as Jesus walked on the water, called Peter out of the boat to join Him, and then miraculously calmed the storm. But couldn't the struggles have been avoided by telling the disciples to simply wait until morning to travel?

This wasn't the first time the disciples faced a storm with Jesus. During a prior boat ride, Jesus had been asleep when the storm arose: "The disciples went and woke Him, saying, 'Lord, save us! We're going to drown!'" (Matthew 8:25). When Jesus calmed the wind and waves of this first storm, the disciples asked each other "What kind of man is this?" (Matthew 8:27). During the first crisis, the disciples saw Jesus as an amazing man. But now, in the middle of the night, when Jesus again calmed the storm, the disciples began to understand.

Matthew 14:33

"Then those who were in the boat worshiped Him, saying, 'Truly You are the Son of God.'"

As was the case with the disciples, Jesus often sends us into a storm for the purpose of revealing Himself and drawing us closer to His side. For it's in the storms where we see God's love and witness His ability to protect, strengthen, and guide. "These {storms} have come so that your faith - of greater worth than gold, which perishes even though refined by fire - may be proved genuine and may result in praise, glory and honor when Jesus Christ is revealed" (1 Peter 1:7).

Our Father loves us very much. He loves us enough to give us His Son as a sacrifice for our sin; enough to give us His Spirit as our guide; enough to never leave us, and enough to finish the good work He began in our lives. Let's receive His love and learn to rejoice in ALL things. Let's learn to look with new eyes and see His hand working around us each and every day. Let's praise Him and look for new revelations of His love, even as we are sent into the storm.

LOVING HANDS OF DISCIPLINE

In the message "Into The Storm" we saw that God sometimes sends us into difficult situations to get our attention and draw us closer to Himself. These storms may be used to teach us basic truths or gently nudge us back onto His path; but the storms may also be used to make major corrections in our course or adjustments in our character. Each is a form of discipline. Each is given with His perfect love. And each should be viewed as a wonderful opportunity for growth.

Hebrews 12:6-7

"The Lord disciplines those He loves, and He punishes everyone He accepts as a son. Endure hardship as discipline; God is treating you as sons. For what son is not disciplined by his father?"

The discipline we endure while in the storm teaches us who we really are, who God really is, and the importance of our eternal relationship with Him. When we receive the gift of Salvation through faith in Jesus, we are adopted as a child of God; "heirs of God and co-heirs with Christ" (Romans 8:17). Our Heavenly Father loves us simply because we're His child, not because of what we do or accomplish. He desires nothing more than for His children to say, "I love You, Daddy!"

But He also loves us enough to shape and mold us until we are "conformed to the likeness of His Son" (Romans 8:29). We are all flawed vessels with many rough edges. None of us have yet been perfected, and the process of being conformed to the likeness of Jesus can be, at times, quite uncomfortable: "No discipline seems pleasant at the time, but painful. Later on, however, it produces a harvest of righteousness and peace for those who have been trained by it" (Hebrews 12:11).

We have so much "self" that gets in the way of our relationship with God - so many hindrances to truly loving Him and following where He leads. We must desire a closeness with God above all else. So much so, that we are willing to pray: "Heavenly Father, do NOT withhold Your hand of discipline from my life. I submit to Your molding and shaping and ask that You remove anything which stands between You and I."

His hands of discipline are always purposeful and precise, and administered with great love. They are never out of control like so many angry hands of the world. His hands welcomed us into His Kingdom by grace and are now there to guide us on a wonderful journey. Our values and goals will begin to change as we draw closer to God and keep our eyes focused on Jesus. But along the way, as our rough edges are smoothed, we must learn a joyful submission to His loving hands of discipline.

TRUST WHILE WE SOAR

In the last two messages we've considered how God uses storms in our life to shape and mold us "to the likeness of His Son" (Romans 8:29). James says that storms (or trials) are used to make us "mature and complete, not lacking anything" (James 1:4). When will all our storms end? Not until the process is complete and we're at home with the Lord!

But there is certainly much more to our Christian walk than storm survival. The storms will continue to come, but we will also experience wonderful victories. As we mature and grow closer to our Heavenly Father, we will see more clearly His purpose and learn to actually rejoice during our times of difficulty. Rather than fight the wind, we will allow it to teach us and cause us to soar!

These times of victorious soaring WILL come! For they are as much a part of God's plan as the storm. But they are equally a time of teaching - a time where we must be reminded to keep our eyes on Jesus and trust the guidance of His Spirit.

The Israelites had wandered forty years in the desert and were now ready to cross into the promised land of Canaan. But Moses warned never to stop praising and trusting God: "When you have eaten and are satisfied, praise the Lord your God for the good land He has given you. Be careful that you do not forget the Lord your God" (Deuteronomy 8:10-11). Moses warned that when we fail to trust God during the peaceful times of blessing, we tend to forget and quickly become susceptible to our sinful pride.

Deuteronomy 8:17-18

"You may say to yourself, 'My power and the strength of my hands have produced this wealth for me.' But remember the Lord your God, for it is He who gives you the ability to produce wealth, and so confirms His covenant."

We must continually "trust in the Lord with all your heart and lean not on your own understanding" (Proverbs 3:5). We must trust as the storm approaches and as the waves threaten to sink our boat; but we must also trust as the wind and waves are calmed. In fact, we must focus on trusting Him even more when the storm ceases. In difficult times, we are continually reminded of our need for God; but times of blessing can cause us to trust our own ability...and forget.

God desires far more than to just be available during our times of great need. He desires to walk with us in an intimate relationship every moment of the day. Let's continue to trust Him while we're sailing through the storm; but as we victoriously rise up on the wings of eagles, let's also remember to praise Him and trust while we soar.

AT THE LORD'S COMMAND

When God led Moses and the people of Israel out of Egypt, He had many lessons for them to learn. While on the journey to the promised land, God taught His chosen people about living a life of worship and holiness; but He especially taught about the need for obedience and trust.

Though we often refer to Israel's forty years in the desert as a time of wandering, their movement was very carefully controlled. God gave directions through a cloud which settled over the tabernacle. The cloud appeared as a normal cloud during the day, and at night "the cloud looked like fire" (Numbers 9:15). The movement of the people was directed by the movement of the cloud.

Numbers 9:22-23

> *"Whether the cloud stayed over the tabernacle for two days or a month or a year, the Israelites would remain in camp and not set out; but when it lifted, they would set out. At the Lord's command they encamped and at the Lord's command they set out."*

During those forty years, God taught an entire generation the importance of looking to Him for their daily direction. When they set up camp, they didn't know how long they would stay; and when they began to move, they didn't know where they were going or how long they would travel. The importance of the journey was in the lessons of obedience and trust - in learning how to follow God's leading - not in the actual steps taken along the way.

Today, we are also on a journey to a land of promise, and God still has many lessons for us to learn - lessons of worship, holiness, trust, and obedience. We may not have the benefit of a cloud, but if we listen very carefully, we can still "hear" His direction. The same God who directed the Israelites is directing us today, and He longs for us to trust Him and obediently follow.

One of our hardest lessons is to understand that God does not need us to move, nor does He need us to stay. God will accomplish ALL He desires with or without our assistance. But He invites us to join Him and witness the awesome movement of His hand - He invites us to follow.

Our Father is able to direct our steps much better than we can direct them ourself (another difficult lesson). We must learn to listen for His leading by drawing near and living in His presence. Then, whether He says to stay or go, we must trust Him with all our heart and obediently move at the Lord's command.

IN SPITE OF OUR WEAKNESSES

In the message "At The Lord's Command" we saw how, for forty years in the desert, the Israelites moved or stayed based on the movement of God's cloud. Being able to recognize God's "cloud" and sense its movement is one of our greatest challenges. For this, there is no answer but to draw closer to God through prayer, study, and worship. He will reveal Himself if we will wait and place all our hope and trust in Him. But when we hear Him call, we must be prepared to look beyond our ability and trust He knows our strengths...and weaknesses.

After His death and resurrection, Jesus appeared to the disciples and many others. He called them to believe, and tell the world of the truth. But with Peter, Jesus took time to speak directly and personally.

John 21:15a

"When they had finished eating, Jesus said to Simon Peter, 'Simon son of John, do you truly love Me more than these?'"

Jesus used a word meaning absolute, unconditional love (agape). With one simple question, Jesus was forcing Peter to analyze his faith. Peter had previously stated: "Even if all fall away, I will not" (Mark 14:29), and even more boldly, "Even if I have to die with You, I will never disown You" (Mark 14:31).

And yet, Peter failed Jesus in the garden: "Are you asleep? Could you not keep watch for one hour?" (Mark 14:37). Peter failed again when he denied Jesus three times - the third denial being violent: "Then he began to call down curses on himself and he swore to them, 'I don't know the man!'" (Matthew 26:74). Peter knew how his actions had fallen tragically short; so he now said he had a deep affection for Jesus - a brotherly love (fileo).

Jesus continued His questioning until Peter finally replied; "You know all things, You know that I love You" (John 21:17b). In this statement, Peter was humbly saying that Jesus knew (from experience) his level of love...or his lack! But even with a complete understanding of Peter's weaknesses, Jesus still called: "Follow Me!" (John 21:19). Jesus had a plan for Peter that would not be hindered by Peter's failures.

As we grow to a better understanding of God's love, we will ultimately face how small our love is by comparison. But let's take comfort that God knew our weaknesses when He called us into His Kingdom. He has a wonderful plan and will always provide what we lack in order to accomplish all He desires. There is nothing hidden from God. He knows those He calls; so let's boldly follow, in spite of our weaknesses!

PROMOTION TO SERVANT

In the business world, a good job title and description can be extremely valuable. We often evaluate one another, and evaluate our own level of "success," by the significance of our title and the importance of our description. We seem to have a great need to be esteemed; and employees have even been known to trade an increase in pay for a more important title.

The Apostle Paul received his call into God's service in a very dramatic fashion. While traveling on the road to Damascus, "A light from Heaven flashed around him" (Acts 9:3). Jesus spoke directly to Paul and told him exactly who He was. A few days later Jesus said Paul was "My chosen instrument to carry My name before the Gentiles and their kings and before the people of Israel" (Acts 9:15).

With this endorsement, Paul could have chosen any title he wished - maybe "God's Chosen Instrument" or "Chief Name Bearer of The Almighty." After all, Paul's new boss was the Creator of the Universe.

But once Paul developed a close relationship with Jesus, he saw Him as one who was, "In very nature God" (Philippians 2:6). But at the same time, Paul saw Jesus as one who "made Himself nothing, taking on the very nature of a servant" (Philippians 2:7). With this type of

81

role model, Paul was proud to receive his new title.

Romans 1:1

"Paul, a servant of Christ Jesus, called to be an apostle and set apart for the gospel of God."

There is no greater title in God's Kingdom than: "Servant of Christ Jesus" - no more significant job description than: "Set Apart for the Gospel." Once Paul understood how Jesus lived and obediently served all the way to the cross, he rejoiced and devoted himself to serving with every last breath; "I will very gladly spend for you everything I have and expend myself as well" (2 Corinthians 12:15).

It's understandably difficult to maintain the walk of a servant. All our worldly training tells us to climb higher and achieve more; but God calls us to love Him and humbly serve as His Spirit leads - nothing more, nothing less. We have been set apart for the gospel, and our lives are to be lived as Christ living through us. We always fall short of God's plan when we attempt to promote ourself and take control.

There are many openings in the Kingdom of God, but there can be only one job title and only one job description. Our Heavenly Father has called and offered a permanent promotion which far surpasses anything this world could ever offer. Let's put aside our "need" to be in charge. Let's humbly bow and proudly accept the promotion to Servant.

CHRIST-CENTERED ANALYSIS

In the message "Promotion to Servant" we saw our need to turn aside from the self-advancement mentality of the world and become a humble servant of Christ. We also acknowledged this was no trivial task. Every morning, we must decide which analysis method we will use to guide our decisions. We must either choose the method given by the world, or the method given by Jesus. It's unfortunate so much of our "training" has been in the method of the world.

As children we are taught that more is better and one plus one equals two; and as we become adults, we are trained to make decisions based on a spreadsheet type analysis. We learn to choose a direction based on which path will bring the greatest pleasure; or which path will add the most to the "bottom line."

But Jesus, as our supreme example, was never constrained by our finite way of thinking. He taught us the correct path is the path of simple obedience; and He demonstrated that one plus one will always equal whatever God desires.

John 6:5-7

"When Jesus looked up and saw a great crowd coming toward Him, He said to

Philip, 'Where shall we buy bread for these people to eat?' He asked this only to test him, for He already had in mind what He was going to do. Philip answered Him, 'Eight months' wages would not buy enough bread for each one to have a bite!'"

I imagine Philip sitting beside Jesus with his laptop computer, frantically entering numbers. After analyzing the data, he points to the screen and says: "Look Jesus, it just doesn't compute. Your plan cannot be accomplished!"

Of course, Jesus then swept aside Philip's analysis, blessed two fish and five loaves of bread, and proceeded to feed over 5000 people.

Our Heavenly Father has given us various tasks for today, as well as for the coming weeks, months and years. Many of these tasks will be challenging and require serious decisions. In our finite, number-crunching mentality, we will often shake our head and say the task isn't practical or can't be done. But Jesus is calling us to a new analysis - one centered on Him - one that believes "all things are possible with God" (Mark 10:27).

When we face our challenges, let's learn to "Trust in the Lord with all our heart and lean not on our own understanding" (Proverbs 3:5). Let's live each and every moment by faith and allow each step along our path to be guided by a Christ-centered analysis.

BELIEVE AND BE RESTORED

When God created man, He gave him dominion over all the earth; "fill the earth and subdue it" (Genesis 1:28). Man was created with a great amount of freedom. He was to take care of God's Garden and obey a single command: "You must not eat from the tree of the knowledge of good and evil, for when you eat of it you will surely die" (Genesis 2:17). Adam did not believe what God said was true and he ate fruit from the tree. His sin (failure to believe) caused man to be separated from God.

When God used Moses to lead His chosen people out of Egypt, He gave them rules for their personal, social, and spiritual life. If these rules were obeyed, God promised to restore His people to a right relationship with Himself; "If we are careful to obey all this law...that will be our righteousness" (Deuteronomy 6:25). But the people did not obey God's law and so remained separated. Their lack of obedience demonstrated a lack of belief that what God said was true.

When God sent His Son as the final sacrifice for our sin, He gave one basic command: "Believe in the one He has sent" (John 6:29). Those who do not obey this final command (those who do not believe) are condemned to an eternal separation. But those who believe in Jesus Christ are restored!

Hebrews 8:10

> *"This is the covenant I will make with the house of Israel after that time, declares the Lord. I will put my laws in their minds and write them on their hearts. I will be their God, and they will be my people."*

Relationship with God has always been based on belief - a belief that what God said is true. But for this belief to be real it was always expected to produce obedience. The wonder of our relationship today is that God gives us His law written on our heart AND He gives us His Spirit to guide and strengthen us to obey; "And I will put My Spirit in you and move you to follow My decrees and be careful to keep My laws" (Ezekiel 36:27).

Through belief in Jesus for the forgiveness of our sin, we become a "new creation" (2 Corinthians 5:17) with a new heart and new strength. What an awesome blessing!! By His grace we are completely restored into the relationship for which we were created - a relationship of love, a relationship of trust, and a relationship of obedience.

God's Word is true! If He is calling, do not turn away; "Today, if you hear His voice, do not harden your hearts" (Hebrews 3:7). Today, if you hear His voice, believe and be restored.

LIVING A HOLY LIFE

In the message "Believe and Be Restored" we considered our need to believe that what God said is true. He said the death and resurrection of Jesus was the final sacrifice for our sin, and that those who believe would receive the gift of eternal life.

Clearly, our Salvation is a gift from God; "For it is by grace you have been saved, through faith" (Ephesians 2:8). We did nothing to earn our Salvation and there is nothing we must now do to keep it, we simply must believe; "there is now no condemnation for those who are in Christ Jesus" (Romans 8:1).

Though our sins are forgiven and Jesus is 100% sufficient for Salvation - though we walk in grace and are absolutely free of condemnation - sin in our life still causes temporary separation and tension in our relationship with God. Therefore, over and over in scripture, we are called to a life of holiness: "As obedient children, do not conform to the evil desires you had when you lived in ignorance. But just as He who called you is holy, so be holy in all you do" (1 Peter 1:14-15). Holiness is to receive top priority in our life; "Make every effort to live in peace with all men and to be holy" (Hebrews 12:14).

So why such an emphasis on holy living? After all, if we are saved by grace, then our effort toward holiness plays no part in our Salvation. The answer is found in examining our purpose for life beyond Salvation: "Therefore, I urge you, brothers, in view of God's mercy, to offer your bodies as living sacrifices, holy and pleasing to God - this is your spiritual act of worship" (Romans 12:1).

2 Peter 1:5-7

"For this very reason, make every effort to add to your faith goodness; and to goodness, knowledge; and to knowledge, self-control; and to self-control, perseverance; and to perseverance, godliness; and to godliness, brotherly kindness; and to brotherly kindness, love."

After we are saved, we live to worship and glorify God; but this can only be done by growing in our faith and presenting ourself as a living sacrifice. For any sacrifice to be pleasing to God, the sacrifice itself must be pure, and the one who presents the sacrifice must be holy. So when we "make every effort" toward a life of holiness, we don't do so in order to earn or maintain our Salvation: we strive for holiness because we desire to truly worship our Heavenly Father with every heartbeat of our life.

We must never lose sight of God's wonderful gift given purely by His grace. But now our Father's plan is for us to be conformed to the likeness of His Son and live in a continual state of worship. His design for our life is that we mature in our faith and worship Him by living a holy life.

A FAITHFUL AND LOVING BRIDE

In the message "Living a Holy Life" we saw that though we have freedom in Christ, we are also called to live a life of holiness. As we continue to walk with Jesus, we are called to strive for purity in our worship while understanding that nothing we do can ever add to His gift of Salvation.

Perhaps this relationship is best understood by considering our "marriage" to Christ; "I promised you to one husband, to Christ" (2 Corinthians 11:2). Jesus demonstrated His love for us, His eternal bride, when He gave His life; and NOTHING "will be able to separate us from the love of God that is in Christ Jesus" (Romans 8:39). He promised to never leave us nor forsake us (Hebrews 13:5), and even "if we are faithless, He will remain faithful" (2 Timothy 2:13). His love is perfect!

However, His perfect love must never produce complacency. We have no fear of losing our Bridegroom or driving Him away, and we need not earn His acceptance. But if we truly understand His love, we ought to be compelled to return His love in everything we do and live to bring Him glory and honor.

When the people of Israel turned their hearts away from God, it caused Him great pain. They were His chosen people - His chosen bride whom He dearly loved - and yet, they continued to seek a life apart from Him.

Ezekiel 6:9

"How I have been grieved by their adulterous hearts, which have turned away from Me, and by their eyes, which have lusted after their idols."

This pain still occurs today whenever we withhold even a portion of our heart. We are married to a loving God who gave His life so we could live; but He is also "a consuming fire, a jealous God" (Deuteronomy 4:24). When we allow our heart to become attracted to the things of this world or controlled by its set of values, we become an adulterous bride; "Don't you know that friendship with the world is hatred toward God?" (James 4:4).

Many of our discussions of what is "acceptable" behavior for the bride of Christ, miss the true essence of our relationship. We are to be passionately in love! Our greatest desire should be to do those things which please the Bridegroom - not to cause Him grief as we live on the cold edge of what is "allowable." Everything is allowable, but what things properly express our love?

Let's keep our heart pure and devoted to Him. Let's abide in Him and love Him with ALL our heart. Let's commit to living the remainder of our days as a faithful and loving bride.

DON'T STRIKE THE ROCK

M oses was chosen by God to lead the people of Israel out of Egypt. Through Moses, God demonstrated His awesome power and magnificent holiness. At the time, there was no one closer to God than Moses. However, even with this wonderfully close relationship, Moses still struggled at times with trusting God.

After being led out of Egypt, the people often brought their complaints to Moses. On one occasion, the people complained about their lack of drinking water; "Why did you bring us up out of Egypt to this terrible place?" (Numbers 20:5). When Moses entered the presence of God with this concern, he was given clear direction for solving the problem: "Gather the assembly together. Speak to that rock before their eyes and it will pour out its water" (Numbers 20:8).

Moses gathered the people as he was told. But rather than simply speaking to the rock, Moses tried to accomplish God's work with a method of his own choosing.

Numbers 20:10-11

"'Listen, you rebels, must we bring you water out of this rock?' Then Moses raised his arm and struck the rock twice with his

staff. Water gushed out, and the community and their livestock drank."

Moses had seen God's power and knew how much He hated disobedience; yet at this moment, Moses did not follow God's command. Moses may have become prideful while leading the Israelites through the desert; "Must WE {Aaron and I} bring you water out of this rock?" Or, he may have thought God needed help from the same staff used to turn the Nile river into blood and part the Red Sea. Either way, his disobedience stemmed from a lack of trust in God.

God still loved Moses and will fellowship with him for all eternity, but his failure to obey was severely punished; "Because you did not trust in Me enough to honor Me as holy in the sight of the Israelites, you will not bring this community into the land I give them" (Numbers 20:12). God's perfect plan for Moses clearly included a trip into the Promised land; but, even after 40 years of faithful leadership, Moses' lack of trust caused him to miss out on God's very best.

God knows our needs and has a detailed plan which is unfolding according to His perfect timing. Let's listen intently for His direction and then fully obey. Let's take the steps to ensure all we do in our ministry - all we do in our family and in every area of our life - is done to bring Him glory and honor. Let's trust Him with ALL our heart and always remember...don't strike the rock!

OUR PERFECT DESTINY

In the message "Don't Strike The Rock" we saw how Moses disobeyed God's command with obtaining water from the rock. God called Moses' disobedience a lack of trust and punished him quite harshly; "Because you did not trust Me enough to honor Me as holy in the sight of the Israelites, you will not bring this community into the land I give them" (Numbers 20:12). God did not destine Moses for failure; rather, He sovereignly allowed Moses to choose which path he would travel.

Nearly forty years earlier, God allowed the entire nation of Israel to make a similar choice. When God brought the people out of Egyptian slavery, His plan - His destiny for His chosen people - was to lead them into the promised land of Canaan. But when the twelve spies gave their report, the people chose the path of fear and disobedience.

God always attributes disobedience to a failure to believe and trust; "How long will they refuse to believe in Me?" (Numbers 14:11). God was about to "strike them down with a plague and destroy them" (Numbers 14:12), but Moses pleaded for mercy; "In accordance with Your great love, forgive the sin of these people" (Numbers 14:19). God heard Moses and was indeed merciful.

Numbers 14:20-23

"I have forgiven them, as you asked. Nevertheless, not one of the men who saw My glory and the miraculous signs I performed in Egypt and in the desert but who disobeyed Me and tested Me ten times - not one of them will ever see the land I promised on oath to their forefathers. No one who has treated Me with contempt will ever see it."

Today, those who receive the gracious gift of eternal life through faith in Jesus are God's chosen people. We have believed and promised to walk in obedience; and He has promised to forgive us when we disobey and even when we fail to trust Him with ALL our heart. But God also has a plan - a destiny - for His chosen people; "For those He foreknew He also predestined to be conformed to the likeness of His Son" (Romans 8:29).

Our Heavenly Father knew us before the foundations of the world and, in His perfect plan, has destined us to walk in faith and become more and more like Jesus. But He also gives us the freedom to choose. Every day we must choose to walk in faith - choose to trust and believe. Every day we either walk down a path of obedience or down the destructive path of sin. Yes, God will forgive; but He also will not withhold His discipline!

Let's live each day in obedient faith and continue to believe His Word is true. Let's submit our lives to His conforming Hands and trust Him to guide us down the path of our perfect destiny.

SERVE HIM IN OBEDIENCE

In the last two messages we've considered our need to walk with God in continued obedience in order to honor Him and allow us to experience His very best. God's plan is that we learn to live in His presence and become "conformed to the likeness of His Son" (Romans 8:29). This means we must listen intently for God's direction and follow where He leads, not just blindly walk down what appears to be His path.

David was crowned king of Judah soon after Saul died in about the year 1010 BC. About seven years later, all of Israel acknowledged David as their new king. One of David's first actions as king was to attempt to move the Ark of God from the home of Abinadab to Jerusalem. David and all the officials believed that by making the Ark a more central focus for the nation, God would bless all of Israel.

This was a very exciting time. The Ark was being transported on a new cart pulled by oxen, and over thirty thousand people were "celebrating with all their might before the Lord, with songs and with harps, lyres, tambourines, sistrums and cymbals" (2 Samuel 6:5). But even during this time of great excitement, God clearly demonstrated the need for obedience.

2 Samuel 6:6-7

"When they came to the threshing floor of Nacon, Uzzah reached out and took hold of the Ark of God, because the oxen stumbled. The Lord's anger burned against Uzzah because of his irreverent act; therefore God struck him down and he died there beside the Ark of God."

Uzzah's intentions were good, but God considered his actions "irreverent." Uzzah desired to serve God by keeping the Ark from falling to the ground, but his enthusiastic and well intentioned actions were not directed by God. In fact, Uzzah's actions were in direct conflict with God's Word.

During the time of Moses, God had given instructions that the Ark should be moved with poles (Exodus 25:14-15) and that anyone who touched the Ark must be put to death (Numbers 4:15). Uzzah served where he thought there was a need, but he served at the expense of true obedience.

We must learn great sensitivity to God's leading. Seemingly godly action, if done outside the will of God, is sin. We must never assume that what "looks" good and godly is truly of God. Our Heavenly Father will always be faithful to lead us in His perfect will. But we must be willing to spend time (often, lots of time!) worshiping at His feet, communing with Him in prayer, and waiting patiently for His direction. As we serve our Lord, let's do so with great enthusiasm; but let's always allow Him to lead and serve Him in obedience.

IMMEASURABLY MORE

Prayer is a vitally important part of our Christian walk, but it's often greatly misunderstood. Prayer is how we talk with our Heavenly Father. It can never be used to manipulate God nor cause Him to do anything outside His perfect will. God is not our magic genie who has to grant our wishes!

Our attitude toward prayer reveals much about how we view God and the closeness of our relationship through faith in Jesus. If we continually wait for a crisis before we pray, we actually demonstrate a lack of love. A man may say he loves his wife but if he only occasionally talks with her, he reveals a shallow relationship. True love will always be reflected by a desire to spend time together.

And if we lift our problems to God in prayer but also give Him our expected solutions, we demonstrate a lack of trust and reveal a misunderstanding of His sovereign nature and limitless ability.

Ephesians 3:20

"Now to Him who is able to do immeasurably more than all we ask or imagine, according to His power that is at work within us."

The consistent message through all of scripture is that God is calling us to a closer relationship - calling us to love Him with ALL our heart, soul, mind and strength (Mark 12:30). Therefore, our prayers MUST begin from a position of love. He wants us to continually know Him more and understand the true meaning of: "My God will meet all your needs" (Philippians 4:19), and "with God all things are possible" (Matthew 19:26). He wants us to love Him and trust Him to provide!

It's foolish for us to limit God to our own understanding. He created the Universe and knew the end of time before the beginning. He can, and will, "perfectly" solve our problems. He is working all things together for the good and using all situations to conform us to the likeness of His Son (Romans 8:28-29).

Through a proper attitude of prayer, we acknowledge and submit to God's sovereignty. We praise Him because we know He is able to do much more than anything we ask, and we submit to His perfect understanding and purpose: "Your will be done on earth as it is in heaven" (Matthew 6:10). Our prayer is not a matter of "working things out" with God - not of wrestling until we obtain OUR solution - rather, prayer simply becomes submission to His direction and trust in His perfect plan.

We must present ourselves as empty vessels and allow God to work through us each and every day. Let's love Him enough to "pray continually" (1 Thessalonians 5:17). Let's make our requests known, but then let's submit and humbly acknowledge that He can do immeasurably more.

BE CLEAN

The term leprosy, as used in the Bible, actually refers to a whole variety of skin conditions ranging from rashes, to open sores, to various infectious diseases, and includes true leprosy as we know it today.

According to God's Law given through Moses, a person with leprosy was ceremonially unclean and not allowed to take part in any form of worship. They were to live in isolation or cry out "Unclean! Unclean!" as they walked about the community (Leviticus 13). Lepers were strictly avoided since even accidental contact would cause a person to become unclean. Therefore, imagine the turmoil in the crowd as a leper boldly approached Jesus.

Matthew 8:2-3

"A man with leprosy came and knelt before Him and said, 'Lord, if You are willing, You can make me clean.' Jesus reached out His hand and touched the man. 'I am willing,' He said. 'Be clean!' Immediately he was cured of his leprosy."

Yes, imagine the turmoil as many in the crowd scattered to get out of the leper's way. Some must have been calling out warnings, others delivering harsh rebukes. But even more importantly, consider the faith of the leper as he stepped forward. He knew he would face ridicule and scorn, but he had heard about Jesus and his faith propelled him into action.

Jesus looked past the ugliness of the man's condition and saw directly into his heart. In the heart, Jesus saw a beautiful man of faith reaching out to be made clean - He saw a heart which reflected the heart of king David; "Wash away all my iniquity and cleanse me from my sin" (Psalm 51:2).

Our sin creates an ugliness far greater than any skin disease. Sin caused man to be repulsive to God and totally separated from His presence. But while we were in this terminal state, "God demonstrates His own love for us in this: While we were still sinners, Christ died for us" (Romans 5:8).

No matter how bad we think we "look" - no matter how much sin is covering us and making us unclean - Jesus sees directly into our heart. No amount of sin can keep Him from rescuing those with a repentant heart and a desire to be cleansed.

If there is anything causing us to be separated from the presence of our Lord today - any past sin, any current temptations, or any lack of obedience - we must kneel before Him and seek forgiveness. Others may turn away and not understand, but Jesus stands ready to lovingly touch us with His outstretched hand and say, "Be Clean!"

AN ETERNAL PERSPECTIVE

The path of a "successful" Christian walk is one of daily commitment to Christ and submission to the leading of His Spirit. Jesus said: "If anyone would come after Me, he must deny himself and take up his cross daily and follow Me" (Luke 9:23). Paul understood this commitment when he said: "I die every day" (1 Corinthians 15:31). Our old nature died when our heart was transformed by the Spirit of God; yet, there remains an on-going death which occurs as we continue our walk and battle temptations from a world which seeks to pull us away from Christ.

But if our eyes remain focused on today, our daily commitment, denial, and "self-death" will become a painful burden. If our walk is ever characterized by self-pity, and our trials viewed as the heavy cross we must bear for Jesus, then we have missed the true joy and peace - the true success - that Jesus desires for our life.

1 Corinthians 15:19

"If only for this life we have hope in Christ, we are to be pitied more than all men."

If our hope in Christ is only for today's protection and blessings, then we have grossly underestimated the power of the gospel. This limited view of a Christian life will always fall short of our expectations. Through faith in Jesus, we have been given eternal life. This means the life we now live must be viewed on an eternal time scale.

When we place our faith in the sacrifice of Jesus for the forgiveness of sin, our life begins anew. But this means far more than a fresh start. In an instant, EVERYTHING has changed. The burdens that were once so heavy must now be weighed against the magnificent glory of Heaven. And our "never-ending" trials must now be timed on the clock of eternity.

The world screams at us to focus on the here and now - on immediate gratification from what we can see and feel. It tells us life is short so fill it with sensual pleasures and tangible possessions. God's Word agrees that our earthly life is short: "A mist that appears for a little while and then vanishes" (James 4:14). But it teaches that our Spiritual life continues forever! "What is seen is temporary, but what is unseen is eternal" (2 Corinthians 4:18).

We have been given new eyes! Let's begin to view our life in the context of eternity and gain the greater hope and power this view can provide today. Let's carry our cross with greater joy, live with more peace and contentment, and experience new victories in life's many battles, as we begin to evaluate all areas of our life from an eternal perspective.

A TASTE OF ETERNITY

In the message "An Eternal Perspective" we saw the need to consider our life on an eternal time scale and to weigh our current burdens against the eternal glory of Heaven. But there are many believers who are unable to gain strength or comfort from this view of life. Although they know the concept, they lack anything on which to base their hope.

This is unfortunate, but understandable. If our view of Heaven contains no real foundation, the thought of eternity will never make our troubles seem "light and momentary" (2 Corinthians 4:17). And while it's true that "faith is the substance of things hoped for" (Hebrews 11:1), we still need some understanding or our faith will never generate the hope which can truly impact our life.

When Jacob was looking for a wife, he found Rachel. Jacob quickly fell in love and promised to work seven years in exchange for receiving Rachel as his wife.

Genesis 29:20

"So Jacob served seven years to get Rachel, but they seemed like only a few days to him because of his love for her."

Jacob worked hard for many years, but the hope of being with the one he loved eased any burden he might have felt. But Jacob had an understanding of the one he hoped for - and this brought him great comfort. Jacob saw Rachel's beauty every day and was certainly permitted to talk with her often. He knew Rachel and probably spent many hours dreaming of her and holding her in his arms. There was undoubtedly a longing inside Jacob which he knew only Rachel could fill.

God gave His Son so we could be brought back to a full and right relationship with Him for all eternity. But God did not leave us with an empty view or ask us to cling to a blind hope. He allows us into His presence and gives us the ability to know Him NOW! We will never grasp all that Heaven has to offer until we see Him face to face. But God allows us to taste eternity if we will only draw near and ask.

Let's dedicate our lives to knowing the One with whom we will spend eternity - the One on whom we base our hope. Let's commune with our Father in prayer and learn of His nature through His Word. Let's strive for an all-consuming love - a love complete with the empty ache which only His presence can fill. Let's rejoice, receive comfort and gain strength, as we draw near and are allowed a taste of eternity.

GIFTS TO BE RETURNED

After Joshua led the Israelites into the promised land, the nation was governed by a series of judges. The period of the judges lasted several hundred years and ended with the prophet Samuel. Samuel lived his entire life dedicated to God. In fact, Samuel's mother dedicated him to God before he was even born.

For many years Hannah and her husband had tried to have a child, but God did not allow her to conceive. The desire for a child continued for several years and became such a consuming portion of Hannah's life that she could think of little else; "In bitterness of soul Hannah wept much and prayed to the Lord" (1 Samuel 1:10).

Finally, Hannah's heart softened and she made a vow that if God would give her a son, "then I will give him to the Lord for all the days of his life" (1 Samuel 1:11). God honored Hannah's vow and she soon became pregnant. A few years after Samuel was born Hannah brought him to Eli, the priest.

1 Samuel 1:27-28

> *"I prayed for this child, and the Lord has granted me what I asked of Him. So now I give him to the Lord. For his whole life he will be given over to the Lord."*

When Hannah made her vow, she no longer desired a child to satisfy her own needs but truly desired to honor God by returning her son to Him. In turn, God blessed Hannah with five additional children after Samuel (1 Samuel 2:21). God did not bless Hannah because of her vow (we can never "bargain" with God); rather, God blessed Hannah because her heart desired to glorify Him with her blessing.

We must learn to consider everything in our life from the same perspective as Hannah. We have created nothing of lasting value with our own hands. Everything we have - everything which defines who we are - is a precious gift from God. This includes our possessions, family, business, school, special skills, and talents. ALL we have is by the grace of God.

And just as it's prideful sin to take self-credit for God's many blessings, it's equally shameful to shun His gifts - to pretend they don't exist - and fail to use them for His glory. God always blesses with a purpose; and we live a shallow life if we ignore His gifts or use them solely for our own benefit and pleasure.

Let's bless our Heavenly Father by fully receiving His gifts, and then by giving back what we've so graciously been given. Let's praise Him and determine to use even the gift of our own life to bring Him glory and honor. God has showered us with many wonderful gifts, but they are ALL gifts to be returned.

REFUSE TO BE AFRAID

As wars continue around the world, we must remember our true battles are not against flesh and blood - not against terrorism or weapons of mass destruction, nor against an oppressive boss or unappreciative spouse - but "against the spiritual forces of evil in the Heavenly realms" (Ephesians 6:12). The real battles occur in a world which is real, but unseen; and yet, the battles we see and hear everywhere we turn are the ones which tend to consume our thoughts and cause us to fear.

As Jesus was teaching and healing around the Sea of Galilee, large crowds of people began to come out to Him. One evening, Jesus decided to leave the crowds behind and sail with His disciples to the other side of the sea. As Jesus slept in the back of the boat, a terrible storm soon developed. The disciples woke Jesus and cried out in fear, "Teacher, don't You care if we drown?" (Mark 4:38).

Mark 4:39-40

"He got up, rebuked the wind and said to the waves, 'Quiet! Be still!' Then the wind died down and it was completely calm. He said to His disciples, 'Why are you so afraid? Do you still have no faith?'"

The disciples had seen Jesus cure a man with leprosy, heal a paralytic, and teach with the authority of Almighty God; but now they thought Jesus didn't care. When Jesus rose, He rebuked the storm as well as His disciples. These men who were chosen to walk with the Son of God were now accused by Jesus of being afraid and living without faith.

This same event occurs in our life today. Jesus climbs into our boat and directs us to a distant shore. We've heard about His miracles so we joyfully cast off, expecting a smooth sail. Suddenly, the wind begins to blow and the waves turn white - this is probably not the voyage we had in mind. No longer able to see the shore, we begin to wonder why we ever set sail. Did we really hear His voice? And in our desperation we pathetically cry out, "Don't You care if we drown?" .... Is our faith really so weak?

In the midst of our fears, we must remember: He is the same God who created the Heavens and the earth, sent His Son to die for our sins, and gave us His Spirit "with whom we were sealed for the day of redemption" (Ephesians 4:30). He is the same God who chose us to walk by His side!

Jesus is still committed to our journey, and still in complete control. In His perfect timing He will calm ALL the wind and waves - ALL the roaring seas. When doubts begin to surface, we must draw even closer, hold on even tighter, and trust Him even deeper. No matter what battles we see with our eyes and hear with our ears, we must be determined to live each moment by faith and refuse to be afraid.

THE SEARCH

We have come to that wonderful place where our only desire is to do God's will. We have begun to view our time on earth with an eternal perspective and are now in the process of aligning our life with His desires. This is a significant step of maturity for any believer, but it can also be a time of great frustration. We truly desire to do the will of God, so we desperately (and often unceasingly) search for His will.

Before we were saved, we were controlled by a sinful nature. This nature manifested itself in a variety of ways; "sexual immorality, impurity and debauchery; idolatry and witchcraft; hatred, discord, jealousy, fits of rage, selfish ambition, dissensions, factions and envy; drunkenness, orgies, and the like" (Galatians 5:19-21).

Through the Spirit of Christ, we now have the power to break free from the control of the sinful nature. And, though most of the sinful nature is clearly out of character with a Christian walk, the sin which is often the hardest to recognize is that of selfish ambition. Even in our striving to live according to God's will, we continually battle the desire to achieve and accomplish.

The deception sounds so good and spiritual: "God, let me do something really great....for You! I'm ready to have a MAJOR impact in Your Kingdom." We look for God's will as if it's some sort of mountain to climb, and then we become frustrated when we never seem to arrive at the summit. But God's will is never a destination. His will is always a process - always found in the journey! His will is that we love Him, trust Him, and seek Him with all our heart.

Psalm 9:10

> *"Those who know Your name will trust in You, for You, Lord, have never forsaken those who seek You."*

Anyone who earnestly searches for God's will has a strong desire to please Him. They love God with all their heart and are leaning on Him for guidance like never before. This love and trust mean more to God than anything we could ever accomplish. But God allows us to search, because the search is what brings us to His throne.

We must continue to seek His desire for our life and always be prepared to follow where He leads. But we must also strip back the layers of pride which require an achievement of something grand. We have found His perfect will when we walk in humble submission, with a thankful heart, and are actively involved in the search.

THE PROMISED LAND

In the message "The Search" we saw how searching for God's will is a natural step of Christian maturity. As we become more like Christ, we naturally desire to do only those things consistent with the will of our Heavenly Father. But we also saw that this can be a frustrating time as we search...and wait! But it's a time where we learn more about trust, more about submitting our own desires to His will, and more about preparing to go when He calls.

Abraham was a man of great faith. He was chosen to begin the covenant relationship between God and man. Through Abraham's son Isaac and his grandson Jacob, the nation of Israel was born. However, when God's Word first introduces us to Abraham, he is already 75 years old and settled with his family in the land of Haran. Then, with absolutely no warning, God calls...

Genesis 12:1

> *"The Lord had said to Abraham, 'Leave your country, your people and your father's household and go to the land I will show you.'"*

God wanted Abraham to move to the land of promise; "I will make you into a great nation and I will bless you" (Genesis 12:2). We're not told that Abraham was searching for God's will or even preparing for the call, but he was definitely ready. Abraham had no idea where he was going, how long he would be gone or how he was going to get to where God directed, but he trusted God's promise and went.

It's interesting to note there was no further discussion or clarification from God after the call was made - God gave direction, and Abraham obeyed; "So Abraham left, as the Lord had told him" (Genesis 12:4). Abraham may have left with a slight uncertainty in his decision - a slight hesitation in his step - but he had faith enough to trust and obey.

God has a promised land to which He's calling us today. It's a land where we find contentment in all situations (Philippians 4:12), rejoice in our trials (James 1:2), and give thanks in all circumstances (1 Thessalonians 5:18) because we KNOW God is working all things together for the good (Romans 8:28). It's a land of united families where marriage vows represent an unbreakable covenant; a place where children honor their father and mother; and a land where parents lead their children by following Christ. Most of all, it's a land where we love Him with ALL our heart in ALL we do, say and think!

He's calling us to trust Him and follow where He leads. Sometimes His call is very specific - and we must diligently prepare to hear and obey this call - but often His call is simply to let go of our own understanding, search His Word for truth, and follow Him to the Promised Land.

BUILD ACCORDING TO THE SPIRIT

When the armies of Babylon made their final invasion of Jerusalem, they took many captives into exile and completely destroyed the temple - destroyed God's dwelling among His chosen people. After many years, a group of Israelites were allowed to return to Jerusalem and rebuild.

This group began the work with great excitement: "With praise and thanksgiving they sang to the Lord, 'He is good; His love to Israel endures forever'" (Ezra 3:11). But they soon encountered opposition; "The peoples around them set out to discourage the people of Judah and make them afraid to go on building" (Ezra 4:4). The opposition grew until all construction came to a standstill.

God sent a message through the prophet Haggai to encourage His people to return to their important task.

Haggai 2:4-5

*"Be strong, all you people of the land,"
declares the Lord, "and work. For I am
with you," declares the Lord Almighty.
"This is what I covenanted with you when
you came out of Egypt. And My Spirit
remains among you. Do not fear."*

God encouraged the people by reminding them He was still with them. He had rescued His people from slavery so He could dwell among them, and He had given His Spirit as a guide and comforter; "They were given rest by the Spirit of the Lord. This is how You guided Your people" (Isaiah 63:14).

Today, WE are His temple: "Don't you know that you yourselves are God's temple and that God's Spirit lives in you?" (1 Corinthians 3:16). The same Spirit who was given to be with God's chosen people of the past is the same Spirit who now fills us and gives us the power to live a victorious life in Christ - gives us the power to build according to God's perfect plan.

Jesus said the Holy Spirit will "remind you of everything I have said to you" (John 14:26). We have all heard and read the truth - we know how Christ desires for us to live - but the Spirit is given to "guide you into all truth" (John 16:13). The Truth is our only building material, and the Spirit holds the only plans. He will guide and direct as we listen and prepare our heart to follow.

God sent His Son to set us free from sin, and He gave us His Spirit so we may live in freedom and build a temple which glorifies His name. There are many in the world who seek to discourage and make us afraid to continue building, many who create fierce opposition. But let's continue the work He has already begun. Let's continue to walk in victory and daily build according to the Spirit.

A GREATER LOVE

In one of the last messages Moses gave to the people of Israel, he told them to obey all the commands of God and to "Love the Lord your God with all your heart and with all your soul and with all your strength" (Deuteronomy 6:5). About fifteen hundred years later, Jesus referred to this as the greatest of all commandments and then added: "And the second is like it: 'Love your neighbor as yourself.' All the Law and the Prophets hang on these two commands" (Matthew 22:39-40). The commands to love God and love others summarize how God desires us to live.

On the evening before He was crucified, Jesus gave His disciples a final command.

John 15:12-13

"My command is this: Love each other as I have loved you. Greater love has no one than this, that he lay down his life for his friends."

In this command, we're not all being called to physically die for one another. This one time action would be relatively easy. Rather, the general call from Christ is for us to daily "lay down" our lives by dying to our self gratification and considering the needs of others more important than our own (Philippians 2:3-4).

And as opposed to a one time event for a select individual, we are being called to daily lay ourselves down - even when others are not deserving - even when they have not earned our love.

We are commanded to love as God first loved us. His love was with total commitment and sacrifice; "For God so loved the world that He gave His one and only Son" (John 3:16). His love was with absolute compassion and forgiveness; "God demonstrated His love in this! While we were still sinners Christ died for us" (Romans 5:8).

The Apostle John spent almost 60 years pondering the words of his Savior and then concluded that love was the one characteristic which identifies us as a true believer; "We know that we have passed from death to life, because we love our brothers. Anyone who does not love remains in death" (1 John 3:14).

Yes, we are to love as Jesus loved. This means we should love without consideration of economic, social, or ethnic class. We should love cross gender, cross race, cross culture, and EVEN cross religion! Without ever compromising the message of Truth, we must begin to view others through the eyes of Jesus and remove the barriers of our love. Let's begin to truly love! Let's begin to open our heart, lay down our life, and love with a greater love.

HIDING AMONG THE BAGGAGE

When Samuel became too old to be an effective judge, the leaders of Israel asked for a new kind of ruler; "Appoint a king to lead us, such as all the other nations have" (1 Samuel 8:5). This request was actually an indication of the sad decline of God's people. By requesting a king, "as all the other nations," they were rejecting God's plan and choosing to follow the ways of the world.

God was disappointed with the heart of His children; but He granted their request and told Samuel to anoint Saul as Israel's first king. Saul was "an impressive young man without equal among the Israelites - a head taller than any of the others" (1 Samuel 9:2). Saul's external appearance was a perfect match for the superficial values of the nation.

When Samuel spoke with Saul, he was quite surprised to hear he had been chosen by God: "But am I not a Benjamite, from the smallest tribe of Israel, and is not my clan the least of all the clans of the tribe of Benjamin? Why do you say such a thing to me?" (1 Samuel 9:21). Saul's insecurities were so great that when it came time to officially anoint him as king, he was nowhere to be found.

1 Samuel 10:22

"So they inquired further of the Lord, 'Has the man come here yet?' And the Lord said, 'Yes, he has hidden himself among the baggage.'"

Although Saul made many mistakes as king, we must not forget he was specifically chosen by God and empowered to do His will. But Saul lived with a great sense of inadequacy and was never able to effectively lead. He continually stepped out of God's will because his focus remained on his own limitations rather than on the limitless ability of the One who called him to serve.

Each of us who enter into a relationship with Jesus Christ as Lord and Savior are also chosen to do His will - empowered by His Spirit to accomplish everything He desires for our life; "His divine power has given us everything we need" (2 Peter 1:3). Unfortunately, most of us enter this relationship carrying bags from our past which weigh us down and hinder our ability to serve.

What baggage are we still carrying or using to hide from God's call? There may be sins and failures in our distant (or even very recent) past which make us feel unworthy to serve. We may still carry the pain and mistrust of a broken relationship. We may have even made a sincere attempt to serve but taken a few wrong steps and fallen flat. But NOTHING must keep us from doing His will. Nothing must keep us from following where we know He is leading. Let's trust Him with all our heart and answer the call today. Let's keep our eyes on Christ and stop hiding among the baggage.

WITH YOU ALWAYS

Soon after the death of Joseph and his brothers, the descendants of Israel were forced into Egyptian slavery. For several hundred years, the Egyptians greatly oppressed the Israelites: "But the more they were oppressed, the more they multiplied and spread; so the Egyptians came to dread the Israelites and worked them ruthlessly" (Exodus 1:12-13).

God heard the prayers of the Israelites and answered by calling Moses to lead the people to freedom: "So now, go. I am sending you to Pharaoh to bring My people the Israelites out of Egypt" (Exodus 3:10). Moses felt inadequate to answer God's call and began to tell God that maybe He had chosen the wrong person for this leadership position; "Who am I, that I should go to Pharaoh and bring the Israelites out of Egypt?" (Exodus 3:11).

At this point, God could have given Moses a motivational speech aimed at building up his self confidence. He could have told Moses of his great potential, and encouraged him to think positively and be more assertive. But Moses' lack of "self" confidence actually made him ideal for this task. Moses would need to trust God, not his own understanding, with absolutely every step he took. But there was one truth Moses still needed to receive.

Exodus 3:12

"And God said, 'I will be with you.'"

The one thing Moses needed to fully believe in his heart was that he was not alone - he needed to truly understand that God would always be at his side.

When Jesus spoke His final commands, He said, "Go and make disciples of all nations" (Matthew 28:19). Jesus didn't need to remind His followers how to present the gospel message or how to fight discouragement - He simply said, "And surely I am with you always" (Matthew 28:20).

When we answer God's call, we can be assured we have (or will be provided) adequate ability. God NEVER calls without also providing the tools to accomplish everything in His plan. But even with all the tools, we're often filled with doubts and fears - uncertain of our next step. And yet, we WILL step. We will continue to step along the path of the world or we will trust God and step out with Him in faith.

Today, as with every day, we must make a choice. As we choose which way to step, let's remember our Heavenly Father is by our side to love us and guide us along His path. Let's remember He has called, equipped, and given us His promise: "I will be with you always!"